Developing Social Equity in Australian Adult Education

Developing Social Equity in Australian Adult Education: Lessons from the Past presents a case study of the trajectory of an Australian adult basic education program in New South Wales from its humanist, social justice beginnings, through forty years of destabilising change.

It identifies the influences and influencers that have directed this change; those that were responsible for the creation of the field in its foundation years, and that were displaced by other, more powerful actors representing the global influence of the neoliberal ideology. The story is told largely through archival evidence and the voices of those practitioners who helped shape the discourse and practice of the foundation years, and who were required to respond to constantly changing policies and socio-economic contexts. It discusses some lessons that might be learnt from the past in order that a new set of actors might be mobilised to promote an alternate discourse.

This book will appeal to students and scholars of social justice and adult education, and practitioners involved in adult education.

Pamela Osmond has worked in the field of adult basic education in Australia since the 1970s in teaching, management and curriculum support roles in the technical and further education (TAFE) system. She has been employed as a teacher educator at the University of Technology Sydney and at TAFE NSW.

Developing Social Equity in Australian Adult Education
Lessons from the Past

Pamela Osmond

LONDON AND NEW YORK

First published 2021
by Routledge
2 Park Square, Milton Park, Abingdon, Oxon OX14 4RN

and by Routledge
52 Vanderbilt Avenue, New York, NY 10017

Routledge is an imprint of the Taylor & Francis Group, an informa business

© 2021 Pamela Osmond

The right of Pamela Osmond to be identified as author of this work has been asserted by her in accordance with sections 77 and 78 of the Copyright, Designs and Patents Act 1988.

All rights reserved. No part of this book may be reprinted or reproduced or utilised in any form or by any electronic, mechanical, or other means, now known or hereafter invented, including photocopying and recording, or in any information storage or retrieval system, without permission in writing from the publishers.

Trademark notice: Product or corporate names may be trademarks or registered trademarks, and are used only for identification and explanation without intent to infringe.

British Library Cataloguing-in-Publication Data
A catalogue record for this book is available from the British Library

Library of Congress Cataloging-in-Publication Data
Names: Osmond, Pamela, author.
Title: Developing social equity in Australian adult education : lessons from the past / Pamela Osmond.
Description: Abingdon, Oxon ; New York, NY : Routledge, 2021. | Includes bibliographical references and index.
Identifiers: LCCN 2020042199 (print) |
LCCN 2020042200 (ebook) | ISBN 9780367689841 (hardback) | ISBN 9781003139898 (ebook)
Subjects: LCSH: Adult education--Social aspects--Australia. | Equality--Australia.
Classification: LCC LC5259 .O86 2021 (print) |
LCC LC5259 (ebook) | DDC 374.994--dc23
LC record available at https://lccn.loc.gov/2020042199
LC ebook record available at https://lccn.loc.gov/2020042200

ISBN: 978-0-367-68984-1 (hbk)
ISBN: 978-0-367-71037-8 (pbk)
ISBN: 978-1-003-13989-8 (ebk)

Typeset in Times New Roman
by Taylor & Francis Books

Contents

Acknowledgements   ix

1   About the book   1

    Introduction 1
    A case study 3
    Terminology 4
       What is literacy? 5
       What's it for? 6
    The 'field' 9
    Who are the students? 9
       Are those students still out there? 10
    Stories from practice 11
       Whose voices are represented? 11
    The interpretive lens 12

2   Preparing the fertile ground   17

    Introduction 17
    The socially progressive 1970s 17
    UNESCO 18
       Social justice 18
       Human capital 19
    Post-war Australia 20
    Election of the Whitlam government 20

The emergence of the Vocational Education and Training sector 20
 Three influential reports 21
Paulo Freire 23
The legacy of the early literacy programs 24
Conclusion 25

3 **The foundation years**   28

Introduction 28
The emergence of advocacy groups 28
 Australian Council for Adult Literacy 29
Commonwealth Government involvement 31
Development of the field in NSW 31
 Collaboration between statutory bodies 32
The Adult Literacy Discourse 33
 Student-centred 33
 Self-direction 34
 Personal growth 35
 Participation 36
 Emancipation 38
 Social capital 39
NSW adult basic education programs 40
 Genesis of the TAFE NSW Adult Basic Education Program 40
 Diversity of provision 42
 An accredited curriculum 46
Adult Literacy Information Office 47
The community of practice 49
 Collaboration 50
 Professional development 51
 Searching for saliences 51
Agency 52
National Policy on Languages 54
Discussion and conclusion 56

Contents vii

4 A new discourse emerges   61

Introduction 61
The new coalition of actors on the global stage 62
Market liberal economics 62
  The New Right 64
The human capital ideology and the OECD 64
The OECD and a new immutable mobile 65
  The media and the new immutable mobile 66
A new coalition of Australian actors 67
  Australian microeconomic reform and LLN 68
VET in Australia 70
  Influence of industry 71
  The National Training Reform Agenda (NTRA) 72
  Competency-Based Training (CBT) 72
  Assessment 74
  The training market 78
Adult basic education in Australia 78
  A new national policy 80
  Integration 87
  Outsourced foundation skills products 89
  A new national strategy 91
  The new literacy/numeracy actor network 92
  Deprofessionalising the profession 93
  The community of practice begins to fracture 94
Discussion and conclusion 100

5 What have we learnt? Some lessons from our history   107

Introduction 107
A search for green shoots 108
  The moral purpose 109
  Acts of everyday resistance 111
  The future of VET 112
Some lessons from our history 113
  Immutable mobiles 113
  Human actors 114
  Diversity of provision 115
The way forward 116

        A new thought collective 116
        Re-professionalising the profession 117
        Research 117
        Adding nuance to the public imaginary 118
    Concluding remarks 119

Index 123

Acknowledgements

The book belongs to the NSW adult basic education practitioners whose voices are represented here, in particular those who so readily agreed to be interviewed for this project. I thank them, not only for the time that they freely gave in otherwise busy lives, but for the wise and insightful reflections on their 'stories from practice', reflections that have given life to the narrative that I tell. I regret that I could not have used more of these verbatim comments to do justice to their thoughtful contributions. They are indeed co-constructors of the narrative.

The result is also a distillation of the ideas of many people over many years. I acknowledge therefore the influence of my colleagues in the vibrant adult basic education community of practice that we shared. I acknowledge particularly the many professional conversations with friends and colleagues that have informed and helped further distil my thinking as the writing progressed and those who read and gave feedback on the many drafts.

My particular thanks are due to Dr Keiko Yasukawa, my mentor and colleague for her encouragement and continued interest in the project, for her generosity with her time and for sharing with me her vast knowledge of the field.

1 About the book

Introduction

In the 1980s and into the early 1990s, a group of adult educators in Australia and similar Anglophone nations found themselves the creators of a new field of adult education: the field of adult literacy. This is their story. It is told largely through the voices of those practitioners who initially established and shaped a vibrant body of professional practice in the foundation period of the field. Those voices change to sadness and frustration as they reflect on the subsequent prolonged and recurrent periods of destabilising change as the profession morphed from one based on social justice to one driven by vocationalism, instrumentalism and marketisation. In short, it is the story of a journey from social justice through economic reform to neoliberalism as the government confronted and adapted to changed economic realities.

Through the teachers' voices and archival evidence, I trace the discursive struggles that have surrounded the field, and the socio-economic and cultural influences, or network of actors that have shaped it in each phase of its development. I identify some of the factors that initially coalesced to produce a system of adult education that valued programs leading to individual and societal outcomes, and I describe the ways in which these values were later discarded under other, more hostile influences as the field was co-opted into the cause of economic reform.

Although the personal and community outcomes of these programs are no longer prominent in the current public and policy discourse, these are still the values that drive the professional discourse and are still the values that most students themselves attach to their learning. Sue's story is one of those that testify to these personal and civic values.

> When you find some success in learning you can be more open and involved in the community. Suddenly I took note of what was

> going on and why it was going on. I had never voted before, up until five years ago which was precisely the time that I started coming to school. Learning gave me the confidence to want to vote and be interested in doing it. Previously, I used to avoid coming up the street to do my shopping. I'd always had this feeling that people might be looking through me and into me. I know with me, when I took that first step, I never dreamed I would still be here, that I would still be learning. I'm a different person now. (Bowen 2011, p. 9)

Stories such as Sue's are the student stories that have excited adult literacy practitioners for the past 40 years, and that have fed their professional discourse. Sadly, they are no longer the stories that are reflected in the policy and public discourse. The public discourse now is replete with references to literacy's link to employment and productivity. It a position that is exemplified in the following excerpt from an address to adult literacy practitioners in 2011 when the then CEO of the policy advisory agency for skills at the time had this to say to them:

> My core argument [is] If by 2025 we can increase workforce participation from 65% to 69% there will be huge economic and financial benefits ($24 billion to bottom line) to the Australian economy ... To achieve this ... [there is an] urgent need to improve foundation skills ... A 1% higher national literacy score = 2.5% higher labour productivity and an associated increase in GDP per capita. (Shreeve 2011)

The focus of the adult literacy discussion is now on productivity and the GDP. The individual stories of adults such as Sue and their connection to social and civic cohesion have been moved from centre stage. The consequences of this shift in the value attributed to literacy are vast, with signs of strong resentment from the profession.

The student-centred adult literacy programs that were provided in the foundation era of the field and the humanist discourse that accompanied them have been rendered almost non-existent by government's priority attention to employment related literacy. The funding that in the past supported what were known as community programs has been almost completely withdrawn and those working in the profession, such as the teachers whose voices are represented in this book, express concern that there are very few funded adult education programs for adults with goals other than employment. Those programs have all but faded from the political agenda: programs that would enhance students' sense of self and their sense of connection to their community, and with outcomes such as those expressed by Sue in the excerpt above.

I write as an insider in this field; the book having had its beginnings in conversations with colleagues in which they expressed feelings of frustration with the contexts and requirements of their practice, in particular discussions around the educational emptiness of the burgeoning neoliberal compliance regime which many teachers feel leaves little time or professional energy for responding to the real and expressed needs of students such as Sue. There is a strong sense that education's moral purpose has been ignored in the interest of efficiency in development of a narrow set of work-related skills to service the national economy. The result is a system of provision that retains little sense of the earlier social justice agenda and student-centredness, and of practitioner agency over the direction that the field has taken.

Those of us who have the perspective of those foundation years fear that teachers new to the field may accept the hegemony of the current discourse; that they will view their inevitable frustrations as individual, rather than systemic. The book is written in the expectation that a critical history of the field and an examination of the influences and influencers that steered its trajectory might provide a platform from which to critique current and future discourse and policy. If the profession is to re-invent or regenerate itself in a way that will serve the interests of all of its target students, then it is important that the events and responses of the past 40 years be examined while the institutional memory is still alive in the minds of those professionals who helped to shape events or who were required to respond to them.

An additional impetus for this undertaking is a personal one since I share in the institutional memory of the field and have connection to many in the wider network of practitioners whose reflections are recorded here. The history of the field therefore traces much of my professional history and my response to it is not a dispassionate one.

A case study

In order to highlight the inseparableness of the economic and socio-political background from the educational practice and provision, I focus on the drivers or actors that were responsible for the emergence of the initial adult literacy programs, and those that were responsible for their transformation. It can thus be read as a case study of the ways in which similar socio-political influences have driven other social projects in their journey away from principles of social justice and toward economic reform and neoliberalism.

As a case study, the narrative I trace is of the field of adult literacy in the state of New South Wales (NSW) in Australia. Australia is composed of a federation of states, with the federal government, known as the Commonwealth of Australia (hereafter referred to as the Commonwealth Government), responsible for much of the policy in the field. The state governments, of which NSW is one, bear responsibility for course provision and policy surrounding allocation of funding. While the field developed somewhat differently in each state, there has been sufficient commonality that practitioners in other states would recognise the NSW narrative as being strongly representative of the entire Australian story.

It is evident that the shift in the value placed on adult literacy and the types of provision that have resulted from that shift in Australia mirrors the story of a number of similar programs in similar Western democracies in their trajectory towards neoliberalism and the 'new capitalism' (for example, Ade-Ojo & Duckworth 2015; Belzer 2017; Hunter 2016; Rose 2012; Tett & Hamilton 2019). Those familiar with other adult education and indeed social programs more generally in Australia and elsewhere will also recognise many elements of the narrative. The field of adult literacy reflects in microcosm much of the post-secondary education field in Australia and other similar Western democracies, since the whole field of adult education and training and of social institutions more generally have been subject to similar global policies and pressures, with similar outcomes.

It is a story that is increasingly told of a number of other industries and service sectors such as health services, employment services and disability services. (see for example, Cahill & Toner 2018). Of particular relevance to the story of the development of the field of adult literacy, and inextricably linked with it, is the parallel narrative of the vocational and training sector (see, for example, Moodie, Wheelahan & Lavigne 2019).

Street (1995) uses the term 'telling case' to justify the relevance of his history of research and practice of adult literacy in the UK. The history of adult literacy in Australia likewise provides a 'telling case' in that it 'helps us see and understand connections and principles that generate questions and insights with regard to other programs' (p. 33).

Terminology

Many terms have been used to identify the professional field that is the subject of this book in the years since it became a recognised and distinct field of adult education. It has been known by terms such as *adult literacy, adult basic education* and *foundation skills,* to name a few.

UNESCO first named and defined the field as *adult literacy* in the 1950s, in relation to developing nations (Jones 2006, cited in Hamilton 2012a). This was the label it was generally known by in the early years in Britain and USA, and adopted in Australia, although the definition was wider than that originally suggested by UNESCO. It was generally understood to include more than just the cognitive skills involved in basic reading and writing. Although the terminology has further shifted over the years, the term *adult literacy* is still widely used in reference to the field. The Australian national peak body, for example, is still called the Australian Council for Adult Literacy.

As the field emerged it became clear to practitioners that what most students wanted was not simply the ability to read, not *literacy* in its narrow sense, but a general education. In their report on the success of the early British adult literacy programs, Charnley and Jones (1979) wrote,

> What the educational world has been calling literacy provision is often, in the perceptions of students, much more akin to what has been described as basic education. Progress in reading and writing was the proximate means towards affective achievements in personal and social life, towards the assertion of self-in-society, and achievements in the literacy skills themselves, even in their application to material situations, came lower in order of importance. Where success was most clearly felt, students were receiving a general basic education and were not simply in classes for the three Rs. (p. 184)

The term *adult basic education* (ABE) then came into general use. It is the term that I favour and will be generally used in this book, largely because of the priority given to 'education' thus connecting it to a wider narrative. Alternative terms have come into use from time to time in response to changes in public and policy discourses. In general, the terms have similar denotative meanings, although they can be interpreted as code for different discourses. For example, the term *Foundation Skills* has come into common use more recently in Australia, as the policy discourse of the field has moved from 'education' towards 'skills training'.

What is literacy?

The major theoretical framework that has underpinned the adult basic education field in Australia and similar Western countries for many decades, and that underpins the discussion in this book, has been called the social practice view of literacy (Hamilton & Hillier 2006). This is the view that has become influential through the writings of the 'New Literacy Studies' group (Baynham 1995; Gee 1991; Street 1996) and further elaborated by the Lancaster school (for example, Barton, Hamilton & Ivanic 2000). It sees reading, writing and meaning as 'always situated within specific social practices within specific Discourses' (Gee 2000, p. 189). Street writes that,

> The last decade of research and practice in literacy has made it apparent that literacy is a social practice that varies from one context to another and is part of cultural knowledge and behaviour not simply a technical competence to be added on to people as though they were machines. (1996, p. 8)

What's it for?

Central to the narrative that I trace is the shift in the value we attribute to literacy, and the discursive tension around that shift: the shift from social justice to instrumentalism and monetisation. The question 'what is it for?' is usually answered, in the public and professional discourse, in reference to the capital that accrues from literacy; a term that is taken to mean, in socio-political terms, the resources or profit that an individual or community can draw on.

Of the different kinds of 'capitals' that have been theorised by social scientists in recent years, my discussion is restricted to Schuller's (2004) three capitals: human capital, social capital and individual capital. Each has been reflected in the discourses that have characterised the adult basic education field, and the ways in which literacy has been understood and discussed over the phases of its development.

Human capital view

The shift to the predominance of the human capital view in the public discourse is central to the narrative of the book. Currently, the common understanding of human capital is that 'investment in knowledge and skills brings economic returns, individually and therefore collectively' (Schuller 2001, p. 5). It is an employment related, economics driven model with monetisation as its central concept. In the discourse of human capital, literacy is seen as a vehicle for productivity and for national economic progress, as being essential not only to the individual's employment prospects but to the nation's economic competitiveness.

The social practice view of literacy outlined above is inclusive of an understanding of literacy as human capital: the world of work is one amongst the range of social contexts which might involve us in mastering an unfamiliar literacy. Until recently, the discourse of human capital existed alongside an understanding of literacy as an individual and civic right. The narrative that I trace will show that it is only since the late 1980s that tensions have increased between these discourses, such that currently the human capital discourse is not only the predominant public discourse, but it has almost eclipsed all other understandings of the value of adult literacy. In her discussion of the increasing global influences on adult literacy policy, Hamilton concludes that, in current policy discourses, 'The good adult literacy learner is imagined not so much as a person with human rights and entitlements, but as a responsible citizen obligated to contribute to national prosperity in a global marketplace' (Hamilton 2012a, p. 18).

Such direct attribution of the economic benefits of increased literacy has received a number of critical responses over many years (Falk 2001a; Hartley & Horne 2006; NALA 2011) and was challenged as early as 1979 with Graff's interrogation of *The Literacy Myth* (1979). Fundamental to much of the criticism of literacy as human capital is the view that the relationship between literacy and productivity (whether individual or national) is more nuanced and resistant to simplistic measurement than the rhetoric would have us believe. Whilst there is a well-established relationship between literacy and individual earning potentials, and between the average literacy levels of a community and its economic well-being, the causal connection is complex and involves a range of factors other than literacy (Black & Yasukawa 2011; Hamilton 2012b; Reder 2013; Wolf & Evans 2011; Yasukawa & Black 2016a). As Graff (2010) observed, the notion of a literacy myth does not suggest that the assertions promoted by that myth are necessarily false, rather that they are only partial truths. Some of the other partial truths that the human capital view obscures are social attributes such as race, gender, ethnicity and social status (Levine 1986). These attributes are likely more powerful predictors of employment success than levels of literacy alone. Critics have argued that not only is the connection between literacy and productivity a complex one, but that the discourse diverts attention from other values that literacy holds for the individual, community and society (Falk 2001a; Hartley & Horne 2006).

Other researchers, such as Yasukawa and Black (2016b), have identified the ways in which literacy myths such as the simplistic human capital discourse have gained the status of *the* predominant public discourse such that 'it is not possible to even have a dispute about what "counts" as literacy and numeracy unless it is framed in terms of productivity' (p. 36).

We are warned, however, against demonising the discourse of human capital entirely, and I do not wish to do so with the narrative that I tell. Schuller and Field (2002), for example, remind us that it is mostly the political choices that are made in the name of human capital, and not the theory itself, that are to blame for most of the 'unpalatable developments' (p. 77) that are associated with the concept.

Social capital view

Although the most familiar term is 'human capital', the concept of 'social capital' has entered the educational policy lexicon more recently (Schuller 2004). The definition adopted by the Australian Bureau of Statistics (ABS) (2004), and drawn from the OECD definition, refers to social capital as the 'networks, together with shared norms, values and understandings which facilitate cooperation within or amongst groups' (p. 5). This focus on the relationships between groups and individuals thus injects a moral dimension into its use in policy formation and analysis in that it sees social capital as a result of social cohesion and, more importantly, as a producer of social cohesion (Schuller 2007).

As such, social capital is not antithetical to the concept of human capital discussed above, but complementary to it and inclusive of it, albeit in complex ways. Indeed it is argued that socio-economic well-being involves both conceptions of capital (Balatti, Black & Falk 2006; Black & Yasukawa 2010). Increased social and community participation are the aspects of social capital that have traditionally been most valued in the professional discourse of literacy (Balatti, Black & Falk 2009; Wickert & McGuirk 2005). Moreover, it is argued (Black & Yasukawa 2010) that the literacy and numeracy skills taught in basic education programs are of little practical use unless they are embedded in complementary social processes. 'These skills in themselves count for little unless they can be put to good use (for example, in employment), and it requires social processes (i.e. social capital) to enable this to happen' (p. 45).

Identity capital

Although the term identity capital has much less currency than the terms human capital and social capital, it is a useful one in the context of adult basic education. The term identity capital was coined by Côté (2005) and extended by Schuller (2004) who included it in his 'three capitals' framework to explain the benefits of learning. He conceives of identity capital, social capital and human capital at the three vertices of a triangle and the various outcomes or benefits of learning such as civic participation, qualifications, enjoyment, attitudes and values, self-concept and qualifications arranged within the triangle (Schuller 2004, p. 13). In Schuller's framework, learning is 'a process whereby people build up – consciously or not – their assets in the shape of human, social or identity capital, and then benefit from the returns in the shape of better health, stronger social networks, enhanced family life and so on' (p. 12). He then elaborates on the model by describing how these benefits feed back to the capitals and enable them to grow.

Falk (2001b) also describes the interrelatedness of social and identity capital. He cites research to show that knowledge and identity resources 'only become used and useful when brought into play through the interactions between people' (p. 210). This is an appropriate framework from which to view the benefits or outcomes of adult basic education learning since it relates closely to the stories that students themselves tell: stories that are primarily couched in terms of identity and social capital (for example Bowen 2011; Charnley & Jones 1979).

The 'field'

The term 'the field' is frequently used in this book as shorthand to refer to the professional discourse, the practitioners and academics who comprise the community of practice, and the sites of practice or programs that are designed for adults who wish or need to improve their reading, writing and numeracy skills.

The book traces the shift in the sites of provision over the past forty years. In Australia this has involved public, for-profit and not-for-profit private providers, charitable and community organisations. It has also been integrated into workplace and vocational education and training (VET) and labour market programs. In NSW, the Department of Technical and Further Education (TAFE) dominated the field in the early years, so that the early part of the narrative is largely centred on TAFE NSW, with later entry of non-profit and for-profit private providers. The field that I refer to therefore is a changing, politically and historically created one.

Who are the students?

Although the students are not the direct focus of this book, they are nevertheless important actors in the narrative: actors whose characteristics have changed in response to a separate set of influences that will not be directly considered here. In the foundation years, the expectation was that the target learners would be adults for whom English was their mother tongue but who had experienced educational disadvantage. However, it soon became evident that the target learners, particularly in metropolitan areas, included many for whom English was not their first language but who had some competency in the oral English language. Many had been in Australia for many years and had not had the opportunity to learn to read and write English. In more recent years, given the demographic shift in the Australian population, the proportion of those for whom English is not their first language has accelerated. Nevertheless, ABE has emerged as a separate discipline, with a separate tradition from that of TESOL (Teaching English as a Second or Other Language), and with separate sites of provision. English for Speakers of Other Languages (ESOL) specific classes are not the subject of this story although, in recent years, the distinction has become blurred in some sites of provision.

In the early years also, there was an assumption that the target learners would require basic, functional literacy learning. Their needs were seen as being related to everyday, functional literacy, a concept aligned with that which had been promoted by UNESCO in its earlier mass literacy campaigns in developing nations. As the field developed more sophisticated understandings of literacy as a socially constructed term, the term has come to encompass a wider understanding of literacy needs and learners.

It is important to acknowledge also that those students who have come forward for (or have been coerced into) formal adult basic education, and who are referred to in contexts such as this book as 'the students', form an estimated small sub-section of adults who struggle with many of the literacy/numeracy demands of modern life. On the other hand, many who would be designated (according to surveys and assessment tools) as being in need of adult basic education do not define themselves as part of that sector of the population and need to be 'persuaded of the role the government has imagined for them' (Hamilton 2012b, p. 87).

Are those students still out there?

A strong impetus for writing this book was the knowledge that, in the shift to vocationalism and marketisation of provision, large sections of the target population are no longer served. There is ample evidence that, whilst the demographics of the target population have shifted, the need for diverse provision, for diverse sectors of the population, exists still. One source of evidence is the stories of student lives and experience that continue to be published within the ABE field. In 2015 The Australian Council for Adult Literacy (ACAL), in partnership with the UK organisation Research and Practice in Adult Literacy (RaPAL), published a collection of stories of *Resilience: Stories of adult learning* (Furlong & Yasukawa 2016, p. 3), a collection that aimed to demonstrate 'the critical role of lifelong learning, and how adult literacies weave through our journeys, visibly and invisibly'. These stories attest to the value that adults place on literacy competence in diverse aspects of their lives.

Further evidence of continued need for diverse types of provision comes from the Reading Writing Hotline, a national referral centre for adults wanting information about adult literacy/numeracy classes. The Hotline's statistics have consistently shown that adults who call the Hotline with employment related needs to improve their literacy are in the minority (Iles & Osmond 2019), and yet, classes for job-seekers are in the majority. In fact, for many callers with non-employment related needs, there is no appropriate provision available.

Stories from practice

In choosing to present the narrative largely through practitioners' stories, or 'stories from practice', I employ the method of narrative enquiry, the term given to an approach to enquiry that relies on data in a storied form (Riessman 2008). The stories from practice in the book were constructed from semi-structured interviews with both present and past practitioners in the field of ABE in NSW, and from archival materials.

However, whilst I focus largely on the personal reflections of practitioners, my aim is a political one: to give present and future practitioners and those responsible for policy development an understanding of the complexities of the field in order to inform their policy responses. I am guided by the feminist dictum that the personal is political.

Whose voices are represented?

The stories from practice that are the focus of the book were selected from interviews I conducted with a range of practitioners. Twenty-one practitioners were interviewed, most of whom had been associated with the field over a long period, although I also chose to speak with teachers who were 'new' to the field and had no direct experience of the earlier student-centred, foundation years. Although most had taught in TAFE, many had been employed in other contexts: the smaller, publicly funded community colleges; private training colleges; corrective services; or as university academics. All had been classroom teachers, although many had later been employed in middle management positions or had gone on to more senior management and policy positions within TAFE or to university academic positions. The strong representation of TAFE amongst interviewees is not accidental; it reflects the fact that in NSW, until very recently, TAFE was by far the major provider of ABE courses and services in the state.

Most interviewees are assigned a pseudonym, with the exception of Kath White and Rosie Wickert, both of whom held significant and influential positions in the field. To attempt anonymity for them in a field where they are well known would be disingenuous and both agreed to be named.

I also drew on an array of archival information to support the practitioner stories and include other voices of the past. I had amassed many boxes of artefacts reflecting the development of the field: conference proceedings, newsletters, curriculum documents, reports, teaching resources and more. Hamilton and Hillier refer to this as 'the grey literature [that] abounds in a field like [ours] and awaits future historians' (2006, p. xiii).

The interpretive lens

In aiming to identify and understand the influences that have driven the changes in the field, I adopt the conceptual resource of Actor Network Theory (ANT) (Callon 1986; Latour 1987, 2005; Law 1999) as a useful lens and an appropriate theoretical and philosophical approach. It is a lens through which to view developments in the field of ABE as a 'project of social ordering' (Law 1994, pp. 1–2). ANT is described as an approach that

> examines the interconnections of human and nonhuman entities ... The objective is to understand how these things come together – and manage to hold together – to assemble collectives or 'networks' that produce force and other effects: knowledge, identities, routines, behaviors, policies, curricula, innovations, oppressions, reforms, illnesses and on and on. (Fenwick & Edwards 2012, p. x)

This would seem to be an appropriate ontological stance for a consideration of the development of a social phenomenon such as the ABE field, with its multiplicity of 'actors' both human and nonhuman, interacting in a non-linear and fluid fashion and shifting according to context and purpose. It is concerned with questions of how some assemblages of entities came to exert power, whilst the influence of others declined as the social project was formed and reformed. Importantly for our story, ANT is concerned with the mechanics of power. As such it helps make the connection between the local and global, a connection that is important in this story.

Hamilton describes ANT as a 'promising approach to use for tracking and understanding the histories of educational policy reforms which are typically sinuous, layered, conflicted and time-bound' (2012c, p. 41). She makes the close connection between ANT and the view of literacy as a social practice that underpins her work and that of many who share her view of literacy as socially situated and occurring within particular power structures and cultural domains. Hamilton (2001, p. 178) argues that 'ANT demonstrates the contingent and precarious way in which social order is created', and suggests that it offers a way in which we might begin to challenge this order.

I draw on a number of concepts and key processes of ANT (Callon 1986), many of which provide apt metaphors for the stages of the narrative. One of the key processes is that of *translation*, the process whereby previously unconnected entities are drawn together to form something new and in the process some of those entities are changed.

Callon's (1986) stages of translation are also concepts that I have employed: *problematisation*, (the obligatory passage point that frames a problem), the *enrolment* of agents into networks, and their *mobilisation* and *deletion* (the exclusion of other entities), all realised through particular *moments*. The term *moment* is used in both senses: as an important event and in its temporal sense (although in ANT this is stretched across time and place). At the point of *mobilisation*, the project is stabilised (temporarily). 'Like a black box it appears naturalised, purified, immutable and inevitable, while concealing all the negotiations that brought it into existence' (Fenwick & Edwards 2012, p. xiii). The concept of 'immutable [or stable] mobiles' (Latour 1987) is also a useful one. These are entities that can be invisible and that act at a distance, from within centres of power, but develop sufficient solidity to enable them to bring about material effects.

The teachers who were appointed to the field of ABE in the early years no doubt felt they were entering a field that was immutable and inevitable, but it was one that had already been shaped by a global network of actors. Likewise, those who entered the profession in recent decades would have experienced that very different field as immutable and inevitable in very different ways. The lens of ANT allows us to uncover the negotiations and negotiators that brought both phases into existence. In the language of ANT, they can be seen as a series of processes of *translation*.

References

Ade-Ojo, G. & Duckworth, V. 2015, *Adult literacy policy and practice: From intrinsic values to instrumentalism*, Palgrave Macmillan, Hampshire, UK.

Australian Bureau of Statistics2004, *Measuring social capital: An Australian framework and indicators*, ABS, Canberra.

Balatti, J., Black, S. & Falk, I. 2006, *Reframing adult literacy and numeracy course outcomes: A social capital perspective*, NCVER, Adelaide.

Balatti, J., Black, S. & Falk, I. 2009, *A new social capital paradigm for adult literacy: partnerships, policy and pedagogy*, NCVER, Adelaide.

Barton, D., Hamilton, M. & Ivanic, R. (eds) 2000, *Situated literacies: Reading and writing in context*, Routledge, London.

Baynham, M. 1995, *Literacy practices: Investigating literacy in social contexts*, Longman, Essex.

Belzer, A. 2017, 'Editor's notes', *New Directions for Adult and Continuing Education*155, 5–9.

Black, S. & Yasukawa, K. 2010, 'Time for national renewal: Australian adult literacy and numeracy as "foundation skills"', *Literacy and Numeracy Studies* 18(2), 43–57.

Black, S. & Yasukawa, K. 2011, 'A tale of two councils: Alternative discourses on the "literacy crisis" in Australian workplaces', *International Journal of Training Research* 9(3), 218–233.

Bowen, T. 2011, *A fuller sense of self*, Victorian Adult Literacy and Basic Education Council, Springvale South.

Cahill, D. & Toner, P. (eds) 2018, *Wrong way; How privatisation and economic reform backfired*, La Trobe University Press, Carlton, Vic.

Callon, M. 1986, 'Some elements of a sociology of translation: Domestication of the scallops and the fishermen of St Brieuc Bay', in J. Law (ed.), *Power, action and belief: A new sociology of knowledge?*Routledge and Kegan Paul, London.

Charnley, A. & Jones, H. 1979, *The concept of success in adult literacy*, Adult Literacy and Basic Skills Unit, London.

Côté, J. 2005, 'Identity capital, social capital and the wider benefits of learning: Generating resources facilitative of social cohesion', *London Review of Education* 3(3), 221–237.

Falk, I. 2001a, 'Literacy by design, not by default: Social capital's role in literacy learning', *Journal of Research in Reading* 24(3), 313–323.

Falk, I. 2001b, 'Sleight of hand: Job myths, literacy and social capital', in J. Lo Bianco & R. Wickert (eds), *Australian policy activism in language and literacy*, Language Australia, Melbourne, pp. 205–222.

Fenwick, T. & Edwards, R. (eds) 2012, *Researching education through Actor-Network Theory*, John Wiley & Sons, Somerset, NJ, USA.

Furlong, T. & Yasukawa, K. (eds) 2016, *Resilience: Stories of adult learning*, RaPAL/ ACAL, Rolleston on Dove, England.
Gee, J. 1991, 'Discourse systems and aspirin bottles: On literacy', in C. Mitchell & K. Weiler (eds), *Rewriting literacy: Culture and the discourses of the other*, OISE Press, Toronto, pp. 123–135.
Gee, J. 2000, 'The New Literacy Studies – From "socially situated" to the work of the social', in D. Barton, M. Hamilton & R. Ivanic (eds), *Situated literacies: Reading and writing in context*, Routledge, London, pp. 180–196.
Graff, H.J. 1979, *The literacy myth: Literacy and social structure in the nineteenth-century city*, Academic Press, New York.
Graff, H.J. 2010, 'The literacy myth at thirty', *Journal of Social History* 43(3), 635–661.
Hamilton, M. 2001, 'Privileged literacies: Policy, institutional process and the life of the IALS', *Language and Education* 15(2&3), 178–196.
Hamilton, M. 2012a, 'Adult literacy in a global marketplace', *Fine Print* 35(2), 14–18.
Hamilton, M. 2012b, *Literacy and the politics of representation*, Routledge, Oxford.
Hamilton, M. 2012c, 'Unruly practices: What a sociology of translations can offer to policy analysis', in T. Fenwick & R. Edwards (eds), *Researching education through Actor-Network Theory*, John Wiley & Sons, Somerset, NJ, USA, pp. 40–58.
Hamilton, M. & Hillier, Y. 2006, *Changing faces of adult literacy, language and numeracy: A critical history*, Trentham Books, Stoke on Trent.
Hartley, R. & Horne, J. 2006, *Social and economic benefits of improved adult literacy: Towards a better understanding*, NCVER, Adelaide.
Hunter, J. 2016, 'Critical re-visioning: The construction of practitioners in Aotearoa New Zealand's literacy campaign', in K. Yasukawa & S. Black (eds), *Beyond economic interests*, Sense, Rotterdam.
Iles, V. & Osmond, P. 2019, 'Ring, ring. Who's still there? An analysis of callers to the Reading Writing Hotline', *Fine Print* 42(2), 3–7.
Latour, B. 1987, *Science in action: How to follow scientists and engineers through society*, Harvard University Press, Cambridge, MA.
Latour, B. 2005, *Reassembling the social: An introduction to Actor-Network-Theory*, Oxford University Press, Oxford.
Law, J. 1994, *Organizing modernity*, Blackwell, Oxford.
Law, J. 1999, 'After ANT: Complexity, naming and topology', in J. Law & J. Hassard (eds), *Actor Network Theory and after*, Blackwell, Oxford, pp. 1–14.
Levine, K. 1986, *The social context of literacy*, Routledge and Kegan Paul, London.
Moodie, G., Wheelahan, L. & Lavigne, E. 2019, *Technical and vocational education and training as a framework for social justice: Analysis and evidence from world case studies*, Ontario Institute for Studies in Education, Toronto.
NALA2011, *A literature review of international adult literacy policies*, National Adult Literacy Agency, Dublin.

Reder, S. 2013 'Lifelong and life-wide adult literacy development', *Perspectives on Language and Literacy* 39(2), 18–21.
Riessman, C. 2008, *Narrative methods for the human sciences*, Sage, London.
Rose, M. 2012, *Back to school*, The New Press, New York.
Schuller, T. 2001, 'The complementary roles of human and social capital', *Canadian Journal of Policy Research* 2(1), 18–24.
Schuller, T. 2004, 'Three capitals: A framework', in T. Schuller, J. Preston, C. Hammond, A. Brassett-Grundy & J. Bynner (eds), *The benefits of learning: The impact of education on health, family life and social capital*, Routledge Falmer, London, pp. 12–33.
Schuller, T. 2007, 'Reflections on the use of social capital', *Review of Social Economy* 65(1), 11–28.
Schuller, T. & Field, J. 2002, 'Social capital, human capital and the learning society', in R. Edwards, N. Miller, N. Small & A. Tait (eds), *Supporting lifelong learningvolume* 3, Routledge Falmer, London, pp. 76–87.
Shreeve, R. 2011, *'Skills for prosperity and the importance of foundation skills'*, paper presented to the Australian Council for Adult Literacy Conference, Melbourne, 27 September.
Street, B. 1995, *Adult literacy in the United Kingdom – A history of research and practice*, National Centre on Adult Literacy, Philadelphia.
Street, B. 1996, 'Literacy and power?' *Open Letter* 6(2), 7–16.
Tett, L. & Hamilton, M. (eds) 2019, *Resisting neoliberalism in education: Local, national and transnational perspectives*, Policy Press, Bristol, UK.
Wickert, R. & McGuirk, J. 2005, *Integrating literacies: Using partnerships to build literacy capabilities in communities*, NCVER, Adelaide.
Wolf, A. & Evans, K. 2011, *Improving literacy at work*, Routledge, Oxford.
Yasukawa, K. & Black, S. (eds) 2016a, *Beyond economic interests: Critical perspectives on adult literacy and numeracy in a globalised world*, Sense, Rotterdam.
Yasukawa, K. & Black, S. 2016b, 'Policy making at a distance: A critical perspective on Australia's National Foundation Skills Strategy for Adults', in K. Yasukawa & S. Black (eds), *Beyond economic interests: Critical perspectives on adult literacy and numeracy in a globalised world*, Sense Publishers, Rotterdam, pp. 19–39.

2 Preparing the fertile ground

Introduction

The teachers who were recruited to this new field of adult literacy in the late 1970s and 1980s had a very strong sense of agency over their practice, as is evident in the comments of my interviewees in the next chapter. Nevertheless, they were not working on a blank slate. A network of actors had already created a climate and context into which they arrived. The outlines of the metaphorical 'black box' (Fenwick & Edwards 2012) were already immutable and inevitable. This chapter will trace the network of actors that were responsible for creating that black box and the social conditions that shaped the early field of practice. It is no accident that this new field of adult literacy emerged in a number of Western democracies at approximately the same time: in the mid-to-late 1970s, under the influence of a number of powerful global influences or actors.

The socially progressive 1970s

The development of this new field had its roots in the socio-political climate of the late 1960s and early 1970s, a period that saw a seismic shift in social consciousness around issues of human rights and inequality in Western countries. The sense of general optimism and belief in a new world order gave rise to worldwide reformist movements such as the gay rights movement, black power movement, the feminist movement and environmentalist movements. In this period of widespread social change, issues of human rights became the concern of ordinary citizens. The time and the climate were right for those with a concern for disadvantaged groups to call for action. The rights of adults who could not read therefore found fertile ground. We can see this socially progressive socio-political climate as a key influence on the evolution of the adult literacy movement.

UNESCO

This post-war period of general optimism was reflected by international bodies such as the United Nations Educational, Scientific and Cultural Organization (UNESCO), in the expression of the value of education to enhance the life chances of people in developing countries. UNESCO had always been a background player in the development of adult literacy policy and provision internationally, assuming the role of driver of global literacy development (Levine 1986). In the 1960s and 1970s attention was turned also to developed countries such as Australia where UNESCO also carried much authority; authority that Lo Bianco described thus: 'Even at its weakest, UNESCO commanded an authoritative high ground, derived from its universality and the elevated tone of its world mission in education, science and culture ...' (2009, p. 37).

UNESCO became adult literacy's first *immutable mobile* (Latour 1987), the invisible entity acting at a distance and within a centre of power. Moreover, it has remained influential in varying degrees in defining the changing literacy project over the ensuing decades.

Social justice

The early messages of UNESCO promoted a humanist discourse related to literacy. Article 26 of *The Universal Declaration of Human Rights* (United Nations 1948, p. 54) had stated that 'education shall be directed to the full development of the human personality and the strengthening of respect for human rights and fundamental freedoms'. At the 1972 UNESCO meeting in Iran, the *Declaration of Persepolis* was adopted, asserting that 'literacy is not just the process of learning the skill of reading, writing and arithmetic, but a contribution to the liberation of man and to his full development' (Belanger 1989, p. 470). This humanist rhetoric of UNESCO quickly came to be echoed in Western democracies such as Australia.

UNESCO's 1972 publication *Learning to be: the world of education today and tomorrow* (Faure 1972) was a highly influential publication. *Learning to be* outlined four basic assumptions that underpinned the document, three of which were to be particularly influential in framing the humanist discourse that informed education policy in Western countries:

> The second belief is in democracy, conceived of as implying each man's right to realise his own potential and to share in the building of his own future. The keystone of democracy ... is education.

The third assumption is that the aim of development is the complete fulfilment of man ... as individual, member of a family and of a community, citizen and producer, inventory of techniques and creative dreamer.

Our last assumption is that only an over-all lifelong education can produce the kind of complete man the need for whom is increasing with the continually more stringent constraints tearing the individual asunder. We should no longer assiduously acquire knowledge once and for all, but learn how to build up a continually-evolving body of knowledge all through life – 'learn to be'. (p. vi)

However, in spite of the optimism that had surrounded UNESCO's 1961 *World Campaign for Universal Literacy,* the campaign failed to produce the results that had been predicted. Many of the projects had not produced even a rudimentary literacy in a small proportion of their populations. This led to a rejection of the global approach and a reformulation of a more targeted approach. The 1961 global campaign was replaced in 1964 by a five-year *Experimental World Literacy Programme,* one of the essential elements of which was that 'literacy programmes should be incorporated into, and correlated with, economic and social development plans' (cited in Levine 1986, p. 31).

Human capital

Along with the humanist view of education, a discourse of human capital related to education then began to gain dominance. Education came to be viewed as a key to economic growth and its instrumentalist value began to take on prominence. In 1968 a UNESCO report titled *Readings in the economics of education* reported that 'within a decade there has been a dramatic shift, and concern with potential roles of education in economic development has swept the world' (p. 15).

Economists had begun to consider the paradox of the success of post-war economies such as those of Japan and Singapore; economies that had few natural resources but relied on their human resources for their economic success (Lo Bianco 1999). The human capital view of development therefore gained further credibility.

In this period the human capital view of education went hand in hand with the view of education as a human right and with an expectation that education would lead to greater equality and social reform. The concept of civic and community benefit as the core rationale for education was not in conflict with the human capital concept of education although this tension was to emerge as the predominant discursive tension in the decades to come.

Post-war Australia

The post-war years in Australia were boom years, with a growth in population from migration, and strong economic growth supported by expansion of industry and commerce. Keynesian economic policies, which informed most Western economies in the 1940s to the early 1970s, argued for strong fiscal government intervention in the effort to bring about optimum macroeconomic outcomes. Australia therefore had the economic resources supported by this economic rationale for a major increase in public spending on education and other social programs, with education seen as the primary tool to solve social problems. The two prominent discourses of human capital and social justice existed side by side in the Australia of the 1960s and 1970s; they were 'blended and interchangeable' in the public discourse (Marginson 1997, p. 42).

Election of the Whitlam government

By 1972 community concern for issues of social justice found expression in the election of the Whitlam Labor government. Commitment to social justice was an important part of the platform on which the government was elected, with Whitlam declaring at his policy speech that 'education should be seen as the great instrument for the promotion of equality' (Marginson 1997, p. 46). Along with the Keynesian, big-government dictum, this was part of the public discourse that helped to sweep the Whitlam Labor government to power. This focus on education was echoed in the first year of the Whitlam government in a report on the government's *Goals and Strategies* (1973) which argued that 'universal and high quality education is a basic ingredient of an egalitarian and open society [and is essential to] a high degree of personal freedom in thought and action [and] the opportunity to choose among various lifestyles' (cited in Marginson 1997, p. 16). Subsequent government reports, such as the Kangan (1974), Richardson (1975) and Cadman (1976) reports that are discussed below, were amongst the expressions of this commitment.

The emergence of the Vocational Education and Training sector

The emergence of the field of adult basic education (ABE) in Australia is bound up with the history of the vocational education and training (VET) sector. I focus on national developments in VET here in order to provide a context for the emergence and development of the field of ABE.

Three influential reports

The Kangan Report

The economic boom conditions in Australia of the 1950s and 1960s, the growth in population and growth in industry all combined to drive pressure to reform the technical education system: a system that had been a comparatively neglected state-based system of technical training. There was increasing pressure from several sources in the early 1970s for the newly elected Whitlam Labor government to establish a committee to look to the funding needs of the technical education sector. The establishment of this committee marked the beginning of three crucial developments in the field: the marriage of technical education with further education, the related concept of lifelong learning, and the entry of the Commonwealth Government as a major player in the sector (Goozee 2001; Ryan 2011). These were not only crucial developments in the technical education system, but they marked the entrance of important actors in the emerging field of ABE. Each of these developments, in spite of the many positive outcomes, was to have repercussions and give rise to tensions in the field through the following decades.

The title of this committee, Australian Committee on Technical and Further Education (ACOTAFE), marked the entry of the term *further education* into what had previously been primarily a system of trade training. The report was titled *TAFE in Australia: Report on Needs in Technical and Further Education* (Kangan 1974). This widening of the brief for the new education sector reflected the influence of international organisations such as the International Labour Organization (ILO), UNESCO and the Organisation for Economic Co-operation and Development (OECD).

Myer Kangan, who had been appointed chairman of the committee, noted that these transnational bodies had been particularly influential in

> changing the emphasis in vocational education from primarily seeking to meet industry's needs for manpower to primarily meeting the needs of the individual person who wishes, within the limits of his capacity, to develop his abilities to the best advantage of himself and the community, including industry and commerce.
> (Kangan 1974, p. 9)

UNESCO's highly influential 1972 publication *Learning to be: the world of education today and tomorrow* (Faure 1972) had a significant impact on Kangan's thinking and the framing of his report. It was to become, in this foundation era, the next *immutable mobile* (Latour 1987) exerting influence from afar to bring authority to the arguments being prosecuted by the actors mobilising around this new *project of social ordering* (Law 1994) that was to become adult basic education. In fact, Kangan included, as one of the appendices in the report, a list of key statements from the Faure Report. Amongst the most potent of these are the following:

1 We propose lifelong education as the master concept for educational policies in the years to come for both developed and developing countries.
2 It should be made a principle to centre educational activity on the learner, to allow him greater and greater freedom, as he matures, to decide for himself what he wants to learn, and how and where he wants to learn it and take his training. (Faure 1972 cited in Kangan 1974, p. 319)

The Kangan Report had foregrounded access and equity concerns and life-long liberal education alongside the traditional technical focus. Its release marked arguably the first key *moment* (Callon 1986) in the development of the field of adult basic education in Australia, preparing the way for the establishment of administrative units and programs in the state TAFE departments to encourage those who had been educationally disadvantaged to engage with technical and/or further education. By the end of the 1970s TAFE NSW had developed a relatively well-resourced and extensive network of provision for adult equity groups such as women, Indigenous people, people from non-English-speaking backgrounds, and people with disabilities, all of whom had previously been underrepresented in training programs. It represented arguably 'some of the world's most innovative and constructive and successful educational programs for adults seeking to re-enter education or employment and for many early school leavers' (Schofield 1994, p. 61).

The Richardson Report

ACOTAFE's second report made specific recommendations related to adult literacy and charged state TAFE authorities with accepting responsibility for developing provision in the area.

> An effective literacy program will almost certainly have to be conducted outside the formal institutional framework. Literacy

task forces of special staff are needed to research the problem, including the methodology of teaching, and to develop and provide programs, materials and kits for mobile teaching of small groups. Ways of reaching the adult illiterate will need to be explored, by personal contact through community development officers, social workers, and others, and by advertising literacy programs through the medium of TV. (Richardson 1975, p. 96)

This is strongly suggestive of the influence of ideas from the UK whose literacy campaign and programs had pre-dated Australia's by some years. We can therefore see the UK as another actor in shaping the early Australian programs.

The report went on to recommend that 'Adult literacy should be regarded by TAFE as a major challenge. The Committee urges State TAFE authorities to regard literacy programs as a high priority in their use of Australian Government funds'. (p. 96). This recommendation to locate adult basic education policy and programs within the vocational education and training policy area was one of those decisions that, whilst it was welcomed at the time, was to have a range of crucial implications for the future.

The Cadman Report

A third highly influential report was released in 1976. This was a House of Representatives Select Committee report, *Learning difficulties in children and adults* (Cadman 1976) which also urged state TAFE authorities to take a clearer lead in developing and co-ordinating adult literacy programs. This report was important not only because of its recommendations, but also because the chairman of the committee, Alan Cadman MP, was to become one of the influential patrons and mentors of the fledgling adult literacy movement: an early human actor. His name is mentioned in several contexts in the reflections of Kath White, one of the pioneers of adult literacy in NSW and in Australia.

Paulo Freire

The Brazilian educator Paulo Freire (1972) is widely regarded as an important influence on the early development of the field generally, including in Australia. In 1972 he visited Melbourne as a speaker at a World Council of Churches seminar, a visit that is considered to be partly responsible for the commitment of many literacy workers to adult education as an agent of social change through community-based programs. Chapter 3 will discuss the extent to which Freire's ideas actually penetrated the pedagogy of ABE; nevertheless, the Freirean rhetoric, if not necessarily the pedagogy, was lodged firmly in the discourse of the NSW adult literacy field for some decades.

The legacy of the early literacy programs

There is evidence of a number of programs running in NSW on an ad hoc basis by church groups or other community organisations and educational institutions such as the Mechanics Institutes and Schools of Arts, perhaps since the beginning of white settlement (Penglase 1988). However, as Dymock (1982) noted, trying to trace the development, 'is rather like trying to put a jigsaw together: in some areas there are enough details to provide a coherent picture while elsewhere areas remain blank or provide little information' (p. 22).

The period before the 1970s in particular have many pieces of the jigsaw missing. One of the reasons for the missing pieces of the jigsaw was undoubtedly the lack of a public profile. For example, Penglase (1988, p. 40) writes that, in respect to the Mechanics Institutes, literacy programs were not regarded by the management as core business so that 'though these were a vital aspect of the program, records of evening classes in reading, writing and arithmetic are few'. It is likely however, that these programs would have been reflective of the welfarist image that Street (1995) wrote of in respect of the early literacy programs in the UK. He described these efforts as seeking to remedy '"illiteracy" as a kind of disease or lack on the part of the working classes ... [which they sought to remedy] as they did extreme poverty by means of paternalistic gift-giving to "deserving poor"' (p. 4).

There was, however, one significant program that pre-dates the main story in NSW; this was the Evening College program begun by Geoff Falkenmire, an Evening College principal within the NSW Ministry of Education and an important early actor in the development adult literacy provision in NSW. As a teacher and later school principal in country NSW Falkenmire developed an awareness of the need for some sort of adult literacy provision. As early as 1956 he had published a reading book for adults titled *Now read this* which was revised and reprinted in 1976 (Falkenmire 1976). Falkenmire's description of the book was that it was 'completely phonetic; teachers disagree with it like crazy because it is too formal and too phonetic but it has worked' (1982, p. 10).

It was very much an educational product of its time in the 1950s. Although details of the early programs in NSW are not consistently documented, it seems that in NSW, perhaps the first centrally coordinated and publicly funded program was Falkenmire's *Operation Literacy* program with one thousand students over 54 Evening College sites by 1972 (Falkenmire 1976, 1982).

In 1976 Falkenmire visited the UK to study the BBC sponsored program there and, on his return, instigated a volunteer tutor program to complement the Evening College classes, as stage 2 of *Operation Literacy*. In this second phase of the program he started to inject some of the principles he had been exposed to in the UK. These included a humanist, student-centred tone in the advice to tutors in his revised edition of *Now read this:* advice such as, 'In the student-teacher relationship the student always comes first. The teacher serves' (1976, p. 5).

This combination of a humanist, student-centred rhetoric and learning environment, and a largely traditional, cognitive, methodology that has been referred to by Street (1984) as the 'autonomous' view, was one that was to be repeated consistently through subsequent decades. Many practitioners were drawn to the humanist rhetoric but were not sure how to translate this into practical pedagogy.

Falkenmire had been an influential figure in the early 1970s and although he remained active in the field his *Operation Literacy* quickly faded from prominence with the strong emergence of TAFE as the major provider in NSW from 1978. However, as one of the early literacy activists in NSW, his visit to the literacy programs of the UK allowed him to inject the humanist rhetoric that was characteristic of the UK discourse, demonstrating another way in which the UK was a part of the actor network influencing the early literacy field in NSW.

Conclusion

The discourses that came to characterise the field in subsequent decades can be traced even to these earlier decades. The actors that began to shape the fledgling field were non-human and powerful ones within the liberal socio-political context of the 1960s and early 1970s. Perhaps the most powerful of these were UNESCO; the boom economy and the Keynesian big-government dictum; the Whitlam Labor government; and the Kangan Report: the latter representing arguably the first key *moment* in the development of the field. They created a background of humanist, liberal education that the early practitioners were able to build on.

By the mid-1970s the issue had been *problematised* by these actors; the problem being the creation of a system of education that aimed to meet 'the needs of the individual person who wishes, within the limits of his capacity, to develop his abilities to the best advantage of himself and the community, including industry and commerce' (Kangan 1974, p. 9).

References

Belanger, P. 1989, 'The final eradication of illiteracy: A mission given to UNESCO by the international community', in M. Taylor & J. Draper (eds), *Adult literacy perspectives*, Culture Concepts, Toronto, pp. 467–474.

Cadman, A. 1976, *Learning difficulties in children and adults: Report of the House of Representatives select committee on specific learning difficulties*, AGPS, Canberra.

Callon, M. 1986, 'Some elements of a sociology of translation: Domestication of the scallops and the fishermen of St Brieuc Bay', in J. Law (ed.), *Power, action and belief: A new sociology of knowledge?*Routledge and Kegan Paul, London.

Dymock, D. 1982, *Adult literacy provision in Australia: Trends and needs*, Australian Council for Adult Education, Armidale.

Falkenmire, G. 1976, *Now read this – or learn to read in ten difficult lessons*, Oplit, Balgowlah.

Falkenmire, G. 1982, 'The beginnings', *Literacy Exchange, Journal of NSWALC*, December, 9.

Faure, E. 1972, *Learning to be: The world of education today and tomorrow*, UNESCO, Paris.

Fenwick, T. & Edwards, R. (eds) 2012, *Researching education through Actor-Network Theory*, John Wiley & Sons, Somerset, NJ, USA.

Freire, P. 1972, *Pedagogy of the oppressed*, Penguin, Middlesex, England.

Goozee, G. 2001, *The development of TAFE in Australia*, NCVER, Adelaide.

Kangan, M.C. 1974, *TAFE in Australia: Report on needs in technical and further education*, AGPS, Canberra.

Latour, B. 1987, *Science in action: How to follow scientists and engineers through society*, Harvard University Press, Cambridge, MA.

Law, J. 1994, *Organizing modernity*, Blackwell, Oxford.

Levine, K. 1986, *The social context of literacy*, Routledge and Kegan Paul, London.

Lo Bianco, J. 1999, *Globalisation: Frame word for education and training, human capital and human development/rights*, Language Australia, Melbourne.

Lo Bianco, J. 2009, 'UNESCO and Leslie Limage', *Literacy and Numeracy Studies* 17(2), 35–41.

Marginson, S. 1997, *Educating Australia – government, economy and citizen since 1960*, Cambridge University Press, Cambridge, England.

Penglase, B. 1988, 'Hunter Valley readers and adult education in the nineteenth century', *Australian Journal of Adult Education* 28(2), 39–42.

Richardson, E.C. 1975, *TAFE in Australia: Second report on needs in technical and further education*, AGPS, Canberra.

Ryan, R. 2011, *How VET responds: A historical policy perspective*, NCVER, Adelaide.

Schofield, K. 1994, 'The clash of the Titans', in P. Kearns & W. Hall (eds), *Kangan: 20 years on*, NCVER, Adelaide, pp. 57–77.

Street, B. 1984, *Literacy in theory and practice*, Cambridge University Press, Cambridge.

Street, B. 1995, *Adult literacy in the United Kingdom – A history of research and practice*, National Centre on Adult Literacy, Philadelphia.
UNESCO (ed.) 1968, *Readings in the economics of education*, UNESCO, Paris.
United Nations1948, *Universal declaration of human rights*, http://www.un.org/en/udhrbook/pdf/udhr_booklet_en_web.pdf.

3 The foundation years

Introduction

In this formative era, the humanist discourse of student-centredness was undoubtedly the most prominent and the one that underpinned the rationale of adult basic education practice for many years in Australia as it did in Western countries such as the UK and USA (Hamilton & Hillier 2006). For perhaps a decade and a half, the discourse, and the diverse provision that developed around the new project, stands in stark contrast to the current discourse and context that defines the field.

The emergence of advocacy groups

The growth of the field in Australia in the second half of the 1970s was due in large part to the actors identified in the last chapter: non-human actors such as the socio-political milieu of the times, the boom post-war economy and the economics of big government, leading to the election of the Whitlam government with its emphasis on social equality and education. This in turn was responsible for the number of influential reports recommending government action on the newly articulated issue of adult literacy, in particular the Kangan (1974) and Richardson (1975) reports. Action towards increased government responsibility in the field was given further impetus with the appearance of national and state advocacy groups, and a range of new, human actors helped shape the discourse.

In this context, the name of Arch Nelson is an important one. Nelson was Professorial Fellow in Adult Education at the University of New England in NSW and Chairperson of the Australian Association for Adult Education (AAAE). At a meeting of that association in 1976, it was recommended that the AAAE should 'midwife' an adult literacy association, and the Australian Council for Adult Literacy

(ACAL) was born with Nelson elected as its first chairperson (Nelson 1997, 2010). He was an influential figure in the early years of the field of adult literacy and remained chairperson until 1984, when he became its patron for some years. In 1984 he was awarded an Honourable Mention by UNESCO for his services to adult literacy.

Nelson's field was community education and, whilst not involved in the provision of adult literacy services, his interest in community development helped to mould the early vision for the field. In his paper *The community development approach to literacy* (1985) Nelson defines community development as 'a movement designed to promote better living for the whole community with the active participation and on the initiative of the community' (p. 25). He had a vision of adult literacy provision in which various sectors of the community would play a part. These included, among others: commercial and industrial firms; employer organisations; trade unions; professional associations; local, state and federal government departments; service clubs; welfare organisations; women's organisations; ethnically based societies; and religious organisations (p. 30).

His vision, however, was never realised, especially in NSW and his conclusion to the paper is a salutary one. 'My general thesis has been that unless a move for literacy is community based, it is unlikely to succeed' (p. 31).

In addition to helping steer the discourse of the field towards community development, Nelson was a particularly important influence in developing the political know-how of the early practitioners and activists and in 'instilling in them the importance of lobbying and making use of politicians' (Wickert & Zimmerman 1991, p. 181). Archival evidence suggests that the access that these early literacy workers had to government ministers was due in no small part to Nelson's networking and enrolling of new actors, and to the high esteem in which he was held in public life.

Australian Council for Adult Literacy

Following its establishment in 1977, the Australian Council for Adult Literacy (ACAL) sponsored its first national conference, held in Canberra later that year, attended by over 100 delegates. Bill Devereux, director of the UK's Adult Literacy Resource Agency, was invited as keynote speaker, the first of many UK speakers to be invited, and an early instance of the range of ways in which the UK was to influence the developing field in Australia.

30 The foundation years

The conference was reportedly a lively one, with a hard-fought contest for an appropriate philosophy to be adopted by the Council. White refers (below) to conflict over pressure for the adoption of a program that had begun in Canberra using a formal lock-step curriculum, which the Canberra practitioners at the conference were keen to see adopted nationally. This was obviously a watershed moment for the field and one that deserves further comment. The following recollection demonstrates the tension between competing discourses which was present from the beginning, and the ways in which the new actors were *mobilised* and *enrolled* in what was to become the predominant discourse of the era. It is an important moment of *translation* (Callon 1986).

> this frantic working through the night to try and counter the moves by the Canberra [practitioners] who were wanting to straitjacket adult literacy into a sort of nation-wide [curriculum]. I think the aspiration was a nation-wide program using their step-by-step literacy program, maybe with federal funding. It was them and us. These were heady days. It was on-edge stuff. And the typewriters were clacking away and we kept drafting resolutions and we knew that the Canberra lot was muscling in and from our experience of working with individual students we felt sure that once it became systematised and once people had to march along according to the lock-step system, all the spontaneity and the real service to clients would disappear. So there was a lot at stake. And the final meeting was very tense and I think I was asked to chair that meeting and the arguments were produced, and the result was that the meeting decided that we would go with the student-based way and that was a really important decision. (Kath White – interview)

Those who were advocating for the lock-step program and the discourse that accompanied it (an approach that Street later called the autonomous approach) were not among the powerful entities at this point of *mobilisation*. They became excluded from the emerging actor network, but their discourse remained peripheral to it, as the narrative will show.

White also explained elsewhere that part of the tension and animosity at this conference concerned the question of whether to seek Commonwealth Government funding and thus to be subject to direct government control, or to remain relatively independent (Searle 1999). This decision to remain independent of direct Commonwealth Government control and 'go with the student-based way' influenced the provision in most parts of Australia and certainly in NSW for at least the first decade. However, from the late 1980s with the introduction of vocationally oriented programs, competency-based curricula and an increasing focus on assessment, the spontaneity that White referred to had begun to disappear.

Commonwealth Government involvement

In spite of ACAL's decision that the field should remain independent of direct Commonwealth Government control, the Commonwealth Government had been involved to some extent in suggesting broad policy guidelines since the 1970s and in providing some targeted funding since the early 1980s. The recommendations of the Kangan, Richardson and Cadman reports, that were initiated during the short-lived Whitlam Labor government and discussed in the previous chapter, began to be implemented under the succeeding Fraser conservative government. These recommendations saw TAFE assume responsibility for programs such as adult literacy. Although other sectors of the education budget saw severe cuts during the years of the Fraser government, no such cuts were applied to the TAFE system (Goozee 2001); it continued to benefit from the economic policies of the earlier period.

By and large, the evidence indicates that the policies of social justice and investment in education that had been articulated in the Whitlam era were continued during the 1980s, in spite of growing strictures in other sectors of the economy. This period was considered as 'the golden age for TAFE' (Goozee 2001, p. 38) due to the continued growth of funding and identifiable role in the education sector. It also marked the beginning of Commonwealth intervention in TAFE policy directions, as an increasing range of Commonwealth Government departments viewed TAFE as being implicated in their policy directions, and thus became actors in the emerging narrative.

Development of the field in NSW

The year 1977 was an important year nationally for the emerging adult literacy movement, with the birth of ACAL. It was an important year for the field in NSW also. In June of that year ACAL sponsored a public meeting in Sydney at which a steering committee was formed to prepare a constitution for the establishment of the NSW Adult Literacy Council (NSWALC). At this meeting representatives of a number of organisations were involved, including the Board of Adult Education (BAE), the NSW Adult Migrant English Service (AMES) and NSW TAFE. That first executive included four employees of AMES and two from TAFE, indicating the close and cooperative relationship between the two fields at this time.

Collaboration between statutory bodies

Most of the remainder of this section focuses on the TAFE Adult Basic Education program, since the TAFE program came to dominate the field in NSW, due in large part to the large number of permanent, full-time teachers appointed in a relatively short time. In this early phase however, TAFE was not the only provider. The significant contribution of BAE and AMES deserves recognition, in spite of the scant available information.

The Board of Adult Education (BAE) had a number of programs operating since 1972, following Geoff Falkenmire's initiative as discussed in the previous chapter. The substantial NSW government-funded Evening College program (later called Community Colleges) was eventually eclipsed by the TAFE program from the early 1980s but did not disappear entirely with the emergence of that program. In fact, its provision as a public provider has existed along-side the TAFE provision for the period covered by this narrative. Rosie Wickert, the first coordinator of the BAE's state-wide program, recalled that

> almost every college had an adult literacy program and part-time teachers ... It was a big program. It was reasonably well funded ... It has faded from the story because of the funding requirements in the mid-80s. (Interview)

The funding requirements that Wickert referred to were the requirements for Community College classes to also have a vocational focus along with the vocational focus on all TAFE courses that will be discussed in the following chapter.

A close association and cooperation between teachers of English as a Second Language and teachers of adult literacy was a characteristic of these early foundation years. As well as the first president of NSWALC being an AMES practitioner, for many years there was an ex-officio position on NSWALC for a representative of AMES. However, archival evidence shows that the two fields developed different identities, in spite of their many similarities. From the late 1980s, tensions began to arise as both sides began to struggle with the political and economic imperatives facing them and differences related to theoretical traditions and understandings began to distance the two fields (Hammond & Wickert 1993). In ANT terms, this marked the *deletion* of those entities from the actor network. The era of competition for funding, as described in the next chapter, ended this climate of cooperation by these diverse actors working towards a similar goal.

The Adult Literacy Discourse

The body of professional practice knowledge that emerged in these early years was, predictably, given its socio-political context, grounded in a discourse of individual rights and progressive liberalism; an approach to learning that came to be called, amongst other labels, progressive or transformative learning. In this section, I unpack some of the underpinning assumptions behind these terms as they have been used to characterise the educational philosophies of this era. In order to better understand what this meant to the practitioners of the time, my interviewees were asked to describe the underpinning philosophies or drivers of their practice, and I searched the archival evidence for practical examples to support their comments. Those underpinning philosophies that I describe here stand in contrast to the philosophies driving the instrumentalist approach to learning described in the next chapter.

This question of underpinning philosophies had been interrogated by Lee and Wickert (1994, p. 58), who reported that when teachers were asked about the principles that underpinned their practice, they typically produced lists of principles very similar to those suggested by my interviewees, principles such as the following:

- student-centred and student-directed learning;
- curriculum based on student needs;
- concern with student as a whole person;
- use student experience as a resource for teaching;
- negotiate learning with student;
- relevant and purposeful learning activities;
- no external assessment;
- learning which develops student independence;
- student is active participant;
- open access and flexible provision.

These key principles encapsulated the essence of the adult literacy discourse that characterised this foundation era. Searle (2000) referred to this humanist professional discourse of the foundation years as *The Adult Literacy Discourse*, a convention that I adopt.

Student-centred

The concept of student-centredness became the principal discourse of this era and was accepted as one of the 'foundational truths' of the field (Lee & Wickert 1994; White 1983). Nearly all of the interviewees mentioned 'student-centred' when asked to nominate the driving principles of their practice.

> Philosophy in terms of how people learn? That hasn't changed over the years. I think it still has to be student-centred ... (Robyn – interview)

The first issue of the influential publication *Good practice in Australian literacy and basic education* (Shipway 1988–1991) was devoted to the theme of student-centred learning. Student-centredness had become an omnibus term for a range of related beliefs about adult learning and this issue of *Good practice* included suggestions for some practical teaching and learning strategies that were implied by those beliefs. It included articles on negotiating the curriculum; Barbara Bee's Freirean-inspired *Women and Work* program; some articles about student-participation programs; and one asking *Do we know what we mean?*

Self-direction

Allied to this is the principle of self-direction, a principle that was also deeply planted in the professional discourse of these years. One of the recommendations of a national workshop held in 1985 to discuss *Adult Literacy and Community Development* (Nelson & Dymock 1986) was that 'all concerned recognise the individual learner's right to share in decision making, planning and the direction of his or her own program' (p. viii).

One of the related beliefs was the concept of needs-based learning which required negotiation with the student.

> Certainly, starting with the learner rather than the curriculum, so making it student-centred and needs driven and all those things. (Anne – interview)
>
> And always the student was the centre. The program had to fit the student, not the other way round. (Hilary – interview)

At the core of the concept of student-centredness is the nature of the power relationship between teacher and student. The humanist and progressive adult education traditions place the teacher in partnership with the student; the teacher is seen as the facilitator of learning (Merriam & Brockett 2007). It was in this arena that a range of interpretations was apparent in the interviewees' conception of student-centredness. There seemed to be some consensus amongst most interviewees that the decision of *what* the student wanted to learn and to read was at the centre of student-centred learning, and that this decision should belong to the student.

However, the concept of student-directed learning and negotiated learning was not universally embraced. Margaret recalled feeling 'always very uncomfortable with that. [It was] very 70s.' She was very happy to be 'freed up from that' when she gave herself

> permission to be the expert in the classroom. We had always had this idea that we were all equal and you do what they want to do and all that, but learners don't know what they want to do and they have come for an expert to tell them how to do it and [I became] freed up from this sort of trying not to be the knower in the room. Because we are. (Interview)

Margaret's acceptance of the role of 'knower in the room' was probably widespread. Interviewees who had professed the centrality of student-centredness to their philosophies of education made reference to their practices of teacher-directed learning and of teacher-generated and -led activities, without apparently questioning this role of the teacher in an avowedly student-centred program. Their descriptions of the classes that were typical of this era suggested that the teachers did feel comfortable being 'the knower in the room' in relation to teaching/learning activities whilst nevertheless characterising their pedagogy as being student-centred. Few of the interviewees spoke of the practical pedagogy that is suggested by the theoretical premise of student-centred learning, apart from the frequent references to the individualised materials (usually worksheets) that teachers prepared for each student's folder.

Personal growth

The 'concern with the student as a whole person' (Lee & Wickert 1994, p. 58) was a principle that also resonated with the interviewees. This was also associated with the principles of adult learning in its assertion that adult education was concerned with the development of the whole person in both their affective and emotional dimensions (Knowles 1990).

> Literacy was a tool for personal growth. If you have personal growth you may be able to get a better job, go to the divorce court by yourself, and that came from the confidence that the personal growth gave you. (Jan – interview)

The practice of using students' own experiences and own words as a medium for teaching/learning was designed to support this holistic approach. The activity of making books from students' stories was introduced into the repertoire of professional practice very early. Kath White remembered:

> When Helen Gribble brought her 'Blokes at Work' series of little books to that Melbourne conference [1978] ... and that generated a whole new field of reading for the adult new learner because they were reading about their own experience or other people's lived experience, not something that was made for them by know-it-all practitioners using graded words and things, but it was the way people spoke and it gave the formerly voiceless a printed voice. (Interview)

Encouraging student writing quickly became an important aspect of the shared pedagogy. Early issues of *Literacy Broadsheet* and *Literacy Exchange* had an emphasis on student writing, providing a forum for publication of their work, for giving a platform for the student voice to be heard. Peter Waterhouse, a Victorian practitioner and one of the strong advocates for encouraging student writing, believed in 'the potential of writing to facilitate learning, personal growth and empowerment in a wide range of situations' (cited in McGuirk 1998, p. 21). Many students were encouraged to write their stories, and many were published by the state adult literacy councils.

This focus on growth of self-confidence is one aspect of the concern for the student as a whole person and was given support with the publication of the seminal and influential report on the outcomes of the early UK literacy program (Jones & Charnley 1978) and that has been noted by many researchers since.

Participation

The final principle on Lee and Wickert's list, 'student is active participant', is related to the liberation education philosophy of writers such as Freire (Freire 1972; Freire & Macedo 1987) and Illich (1973), a philosophy that was prevalent in the early foundation era of the field and that Jurmo (1989) describes as involving *active* participation, with learners having 'higher degrees of control, responsibility and reward vis-à-vis program activities' (p. 17). Interview data and archival material highlight the active position that the student played in the professional discourse of these early years, including genuine attempts to turn the discourse of participatory education into practical effect.

Kath White, who had been a keen supporter of student participation and who was instrumental in the formation of a student club, reflected that she was

> wonderfully privileged to have been involved in those heady days of set-up ... Things like the student wing, the way the student club started and having the student stream at the national conference ... It was very participatory. (Interview)

The Adult Literacy Students' Club also produced a student newsletter and organised their own conferences. Judith described a student conference at Petersham college of TAFE:

> It was actually very big, there were a hundred and something students there. They actually had a committee and they ran it. I was a consultant and that was the role I took. They basically ran it. (Interview)

Early archival records of the NSW Adult Literacy Council show that there was an ex-officio student representative on the council executive for many years, and a report in the September 1980 edition of *Literacy Exchange* notes that a student representative was included in a delegation that was formed to make representation to the Minister for Education to lobby for increased provision. The early journals of the NSW Adult Literacy Council had a section devoted to student writing, a section that was edited for some years by Maureen Milner, herself a literacy student. State and national conferences regularly had a student stream, organised by a committee of students.

Hilary remembered having students on the committee of her community literacy program.

> Indeed, we had student members on our committee but less and less as the years went by; it was very difficult to get any of them to front up. (Interview)

However, as with the concept of student-directed learning, some practitioners were not convinced of its value.

> It gets back a bit to teacher as knower thing. I think I thought it felt a bit tokenistic. I didn't do it. I could certainly see a role for students who wanted to be involved, but you had to dig them out. I didn't like to do that. (Margaret – interview)

These may have been tokenistic gestures that touched only a very small proportion of the hundreds of students in programs throughout the state, but they are practical exemplars of the rhetoric of participatory education that was evident in the adult education field in general in that era.

Emancipation

Although not nominated in Lee and Wickert's list of principles, but related to participatory education, Brazilian educator Paulo Freire's ideals of liberationist or emancipatory literacy were present in very many journal articles and conference proceedings, and mentioned by many of the interviewees who had been active in this era. These concepts were prominent in the professional discourse for some decades, but with a range of interpretations of what that might mean in affluent, democratic Australia.

> I read Freire omnivorously in those first years. I said ... 'can we call ourselves Freireans when we live in an affluent society? We are aiming at emancipation but surely it is a different kind of emancipation?' (Hilary – interview)
>
> But for me emancipation is giving people the literacy and learning skills to make their own decisions. To me it is not a community thing that he [Freire] was on about. It is a personal thing ... I think we always have used it in a different sense. We still want people to be able to determine their own lives – to have enough skills to be able to do that. I think that's really important. And that the skills we give them are transferrable, that they're not narrow skills like domesticating skills, like Macdonald's training as opposed to a broad liberating training. (Margaret – interview)

Freire's liberation philosophy had been an important influence on the early development of the field in the UK and other Western societies. Although the interview and archival evidence shows that Freirean ideals of progressive and emancipatory education were prominent in the professional rhetoric of the era, there was little evidence that these ideals were translated into practice, except in a very few instances (for example, Bee 1990). This limited place of Freirean-inspired emancipatory practice is not peculiar to Australia, but was a conundrum that similar Western societies had grappled with (Duckworth & Ade-Ojo 2016; Papen 2005). (See also Black 2018; Black & Bee 2018.)

The connection to feminism is an association that has been noted by many writers (for example Sanguinetti 1992; White 1978) and is likewise connected to ideals of emancipatory education. Writing in the formative years of the field in Australia, White wrote of the influence of feminist philosophy which the largely female workforce brought to the professional discourse: 'In a feminised workforce such as that which I have been part of, the feminist perspective of second wave feminists has inevitably made its way into the philosophical stance of participants' (1978, p. 44).

Jan echoed this connection with feminism in her interpretation of the term *emancipation*.

> I see that as the feminist emancipation stuff. The argument was that if you got the confidence then you could take on the world in a more outgoing way, so that you could be emancipated from your ... assuming that you were lacking in confidence and self-esteem, which most of the people were. (Interview)

Social capital

Although the term social capital was not in currency in this period, much of the discourse, including many programs, had many of the characteristics that became articulated as the social capital discourse some decades later. For example, in reflecting on the programs of the 1980s Anne described the ways in which adult literacy practitioners had worked with other community agencies in the western suburbs of Sydney.

> I would also probably add in something about community development. It was, I guess a social capital kind of view – that you weren't just developing the individual, you were helping to develop the community ... [In Liverpool] the literacy teachers and head teachers and Outreach coordinators would be setting up classes here, there and everywhere and going to [local government] Council meetings and there would be kind of, community development meetings, I guess facilitated by the Council with health people and education people and settlement workers and Aboriginal people and all of that going on, and there was again that sort of web of information. Literacy was seen as being part of a developing community and the developing community in turn fed into the literacy programs. (Interview)

NSW adult basic education programs

The development of the field in each state in Australia has differed. However, in NSW the state government took greater responsibility for funding than the state governments of other states. 1977 saw the appointment of the first full-time adult literacy practitioner in the department of Technical and Further Education (TAFE) NSW. The NSW department of TAFE had taken up the specific challenge of the Richardson (1975) report enthusiastically and within a very short time had appointed a large number of permanent adult basic education teachers in TAFE colleges throughout the state, all supported by a relatively well-resourced infrastructure.

The fact that TAFE NSW was soon to become the major provider of adult basic education programs and the major employer of practitioners in the field facilitated the resultant integration of adult basic education into the vocational education and training (VET) sector, a sector that was to become a key actor in the 'project of social re-ordering' of the field.

Genesis of the TAFE NSW Adult Basic Education Program

This part of the story belongs to Kath White, an important actor of the foundation era. Although other interviewees reported here have been given a pseudonym, White has not, since she holds a significant position as the first adult literacy practitioner employed by TAFE NSW and later as the foundation coordinator of the Adult Literacy Information Office (ALIO).

As a teacher of Higher School Certificate (HSC) English to mature aged students at Ultimo campus of TAFE in central Sydney, she was co-opted to help develop a literacy and numeracy Individual Learning Centre which had opened there in 1976.

> We produced self-help cards and things so that a person could go to the filing cabinet or one of the supervising teachers, and they could work at something at their own pace and we would look over their shoulder and help them. It became obvious very soon that we were getting people who were not literate at all ... I remember going to Terry [Tobin, associate director] who was very approachable, and said I would like to work with those people who are unable to read and write at all or adequately and I would like to go to England because I had heard about the BBC adult literacy scheme, so I asked if I could go to look at the English model and then try to introduce something similar. Terry agreed. (Interview)

During this self-funded tour of the fledgling programs in UK, White studied the BBC program and a number of programs in London, Dorset and Liverpool.

> They were using a model using volunteers. They were meeting in hotels, in pubs or in libraries, they were using community facilities, they were training volunteers from the community. They had a schema for introducing literacy. The BBC teaching materials had almost a Freirean approach without its political intent. It was a good program. I took back also their volunteer tutor training manuals. (Interview)

On her return at the beginning of 1977, White was appointed as Adult Literacy Officer to a TAFE college in an inner-city suburb of Sydney to coordinate a program using volunteer tutors, using the British model that she had been introduced to. The amount of professional agency afforded to White in developing this program is something foreign to current practitioners and was a reflection of the professional culture of the time. She recalled that:

> There was an openness to innovation ... so it was a time of ferment, of new thinking directed I think with a compassionate empowerment towards those who for some reason or other had missed out. (Interview)

White is referring here to the culturally liberal milieu of this period that was referred to in the previous chapter as an important actor in this early development of the field.

Personalities also matter at such times and it was perhaps fortunate that Terry Tobin, TAFE's Assistant Director of Schools responsible for TAFE's entry into this new field, was particularly open to this 'new thinking'.

> There was an openness in TAFE policy ... Whoever was the director at the time, he was a very good director ... a very approachable, humane man who encouraged Terry's commitment to egalitarian education. I had freedom to do whatever I wished, with Terry's approval and the director's knowledge. I chose to use the BBC model pretty well unchanged. (Kath – interview)

White offers a further reason for the influence of the UK provision on that of NSW: that is, the ready availability of the UK resource material in that pre-digital age. Although there had been comparable developments, including the use of volunteers, in the USA and Canada, the literature in which they had been reviewed at the time was not as accessible to Australians as was the English material. Furthermore, it is unsurprising that Australia's new adult literacy movement should be influenced by Britain, given the very strong influence that British adult educators had had on the development of adult education in general since colonial times. Whitelock (1974, p. 3) refers in particular to the 'Great Tradition' of British liberal adult education of which Australia was an inheritor.

Diversity of provision

The volunteer tutor program

The model of provision that White first introduced to TAFE NSW was a volunteer tutor model, a model that was widely used in all states in Australia in the early years. Since this model of provision was adapted from the UK model, much of the rhetoric and justification that supported it, as well as the organisational aspects of the program, were borrowed from the UK.

The use of volunteer tutors was chosen, not necessarily because it was cheap, but because it was considered to be educationally well suited to the needs of the target group of learners and to be consistent with many of the principles of adult learning (for example Knowles 1990) that were becoming central to the discourse. The role of the volunteer tutor in fostering growth in self-confidence is one that was frequently stressed. The *person* of the tutor was believed to be the primary factor that they brought to the tutoring situation, rather than formal teaching qualifications.

This growth in the popularity of non-professionalised education came in the wake of the deschooling movement of the 1960s and 1970s (for example Holt 1976; Neill 1968) and its disenchantment with institutionalised education. A report by the Victorian Centre for Adult Education highlighted this connection, with the statement that the centre's volunteer network 'epitomises the deschooling concept; it is flexible, informal, warm and operates where people are' (cited in White 1978, p. 42).

Paulo Freire's (1972) liberationist philosophy provided a further philosophical justification for the use of literacy volunteers. Freire saw institutional education as fostering 'domestication' rather than 'liberation'. The use of non-professionalised tutors was regarded as enabling the process that Freire (1972) referred to as conscientisation, or becoming conscious of the forces that control their lives in order to become empowered, since tutors and students were able to engage in dialogue about issues of personal and political importance. I am not sure that this happened in many instances, but it was part of the rhetoric.

Along with these pedagogical reasons for the adoption of volunteer tutor programs, a further argument related to the increased social capital that such programs brought. White cites the references to community involvement in the UK publications of the adult literacy movement, such as claims that voluntarism is 'a living indication of the caring community', and that volunteers demonstrate 'the caring nature of the community' (White 1978, p. 42).

White and Gribble (1986) wrote that voluntarism is the expression of 'a belief in our common humanity and the importance of finding ways whereby that humanity can be expressed through sharing and caring so that the humanity of both giver and receiver grows and flourishes' (p. 44).

Class-based tuition

In spite of the prominence of volunteer tutor programs in these early years, they were never viewed as the sole or even optimum response to the needs of all. Two years after Kath White and the first Adult Literacy Officers were appointed to develop and manage volunteer tutor programs throughout the state, TAFE NSW appointed the first adult basic education teachers, whose role was to teach small group classes with a student:teacher ratio of 6:1 and within a very short time were being offered in nearly every TAFE college in the state alongside and complementary to the volunteer tutor programs. They were usually conducted on TAFE campuses, although many were conducted in community centres and other off-campus locations.

Most interviewees agreed that the low student:teacher ratio allowed for student-centred learning and fulfilled many of the humanist requirements for adult literacy provision that the advocates of 1:1 tuition claimed for that mode, such as individualised tuition. In general, 1:1 tuition was the favoured mode if the student was very anxious about returning to what he or she perceived as being a school-like environment, or where there was no class-based tuition available at an appropriate time or place. However, it gradually came to be accepted that class-based tuition had added benefits that the group dynamics provided, and the move from 1:1 to class provision was seen to be a desirable progression once the student had developed in self-confidence. Brigid recalled arriving at a conviction that was typical of the feelings of many teachers:

And I used to go and give lessons [myself] once a week to a woman in a caravan park ... and I used to go to migrant homes of women who were too frightened to come into the college but I very soon began to see that they could be offered a whole lot more in the college, in the group situation ... I just came to the position that a well-funded class where there could be some group and individual [work] and keep it small was where the ideal work happened. (Interview)

The emergence of tensions

Although both modes of tuition were widely seen to be complementary, within a few years tensions began to be felt between the advocates and opponents of the volunteer tutor scheme. During 1986 and 1987 a controversy arose over whether volunteer tutor programs had any place in the NSW TAFE program. In October 1986 the TAFE Teachers Association (TAFE TA) of the NSW Teachers Federation passed the following resolution which was overwhelmingly carried:

That TAFE TA reaffirms its opposition to the use of [literacy] volunteers ... We do not believe they provide an adequate quality of service for students. We are opposed to the use of volunteers in colleges both educationally and industrially. (NSW Adult Literacy Council 1987, p. 3)

The industrial issue had come to the fore largely in response to the first wave of newly qualified graduates with specialist qualifications from the Institute of Technical and Adult Teacher Education (later to become the University of Technology Sydney) and from other tertiary institutions in the country. For the first time there was a pool of appropriately qualified and under-employed adult basic education teachers and the field now had a firm academic basis. Conflict with the volunteer tutor program seemed to be an inevitability.

Underpinning this argument against volunteers and in favour of a professionalised provision was the feeling that volunteerism was suggestive of a charity model of provision, a relic of the 19th century middle class paternalistic attitude of 'help for these poor people' (Street 1995). The feeling was expressed that this association with voluntarism was hindering acceptance of the field into the mainstream of adult education (Campbell 2009).

Many of my interviewees reflected on this as a tense and bruising time. Meetings were held and papers and submissions were written, while the TAFE manager responsible for adult basic education policy considered an appropriate response. The argument in favour of preserving a diversity of provision and therefore preserving the option of a volunteer tutor program was the argument that eventually prevailed. The NSW Adult Literacy Council's conclusion to their discussion paper on the issue was that 'reducing the choice of learning opportunities for adult non-readers cannot be supported on any grounds' (1987, p. 6).

This need for diversity of programs was supported at government level also, for example by the Commonwealth Tertiary Education Commission (CTEC), the body through which Commonwealth funding to the states was channelled. A report of the Commission in 1984, in addressing the need for an adult literacy campaign, made recommendations concerning the need for diversity of provision and 'the need for more full-time permanent staff and the importance of substantial professional support for volunteer tutors' (Wickert & Zimmerman 1991, p. 184). At this time the policy discourse was in agreement with the professional discourse.

The high point in the use of volunteer tutors was reached in the late 1980s. However, decline in the number of TAFE Adult Literacy Officers and the volunteer programs they supported began from that time as ABE provision began to be progressively professionalised and enveloped within the VET system.

The perceived cost of the program was seen to be another reason for its demise. Although White and Gribble estimated that the cost of a properly supported volunteer tutor program approximated the cost of a full-time teacher teaching small group classes (1986, p. 50), it seems that an Adult Literacy Officer's program did not represent value for money in TAFE's complex system for allocation of funds.

It is apparent also that the increased funding to the VET sector and to ABE in general in the late 1980s played a major role in the bureaucratisation of the adult literacy field as accountability and cost effectiveness became the major focus of educational programs, as will be further discussed in the following chapter. The community-based work of Adult Literacy Officers, offering tuition through volunteers, was an uneasy fit with TAFE's increasingly stringent accountability measures.

The phasing out of the volunteer tutor program was perhaps the first of many demonstrations that the bureaucratic structures and procedures of an institution such as TAFE had become ultimately incompatible with the requirements of a humanist, student-centred program. At the time of writing, there are very few, if any, volunteer tutor programs in TAFE NSW, nor have there been for some time.

An accredited curriculum

In the formative years of the adult basic education program there were no mandated curricula, and therefore no assessment protocols, allowing teachers to devise their own teaching programs and strategies to meet individual student needs. This placing of the program outside of the formal educational frameworks was considered by very many to be its strength. However, many felt that some students were wanting more than this part-time 'at the fringes' provision. In response to this need, a new full-time course called *Starting Points* was developed in 1986 (Hazell 1998), offering two subjects that would be a pathway to TAFE's equivalent of high school year 10. This was the beginning of the concept of articulation from adult basic education to other formalised technical or further education programs.

In 1989 *Starting Points* became formalised into TAFE's first accredited adult basic education course, the *Certificate of Adult Basic Education* (CABE). It became organised into a full-time program that included vocationally oriented subjects as well as general education subjects. Helen Kebby, who was part of the implementation team, described the efforts to make the course responsive to students' needs and interests:

> It is difficult to describe the content of the course as it varies considerably depending on where the course is being run, who the students are and the interests and goals they have, and the special talents of the teachers and so forth. (Kebby 1989, p. 15)

Kebby wrote of the underpinning adult education principle of drawing on the students' experience and wealth of interests in order to make the learning experience relevant and meaningful. For this reason, teachers were required to negotiate the content of the subjects with the students.

The core subjects of Literacy and Maths had externally set components and assessment tasks, which caused some concern amongst practitioners, as Kebby recalled:

> There was a huge outcry about the imposition of assessment ... It was seen as radical and a sell out to ABE learners to do assessment. We were seen to be pushing a structure on failed school learners. (Hazell 1998, p. 13)

Brigid agreed that the assessment aspect of CABE was the one that caused most concern.

We began to be confronted with a whole lot of accountability measures that really were counteractive to why the people had come there, and that dilemma was never gotten over. (Interview)

On the other hand, some of the teachers I interviewed were grudgingly accepting of it and fitted it into their philosophy of what adult basic education was about. When asked if CABE and its later iterations changed any aspects of her practice, Jan replied 'No, no, that was very much just – keep doing what you were doing and change the wording on your reporting documents'. Most of the interviewees agreed.

That was a very interesting time because we moved out of the totally individually based program to a structural syllabus based project but it was always around manipulating things to suit what you wanted the outcome to be. (Joanne – interview)

It was something quite different to what we had all been practicing previously and I remember it being simultaneously exciting and simultaneously it was a bit of a sense of – oooh how are we going to make that suit everybody? But of course, we did – and I think that was possibly the beginning of 20 or 30 years of finding ways to get around or to twist or interpret documents to suit our learners which is what our game is all about. (Anne – interview)

This was perhaps the first evidence of teacher resistance (Tusting 2009) to an alien professional discourse.

Some however, were not as comfortable with the bigger class sizes that resulted from this accredited curriculum, with their school associations. Brigid felt she was:

not as comfortable I guess – the bigger the class got and the more like the traditional ... Because I mean, what I loved was the satisfaction of helping individuals with their individual lives. (Interview)

Adult Literacy Information Office

Another important example of the educational context of the late 1970s was the establishment of the Adult Literacy Information Office (ALIO) in Sydney in 1979. ALIO was established as a referral and resource agency and professional development centre for the field in NSW, loosely following the model of Britain's Adult Literacy Resource Agency. Its first coordinator was Kath White, who with a number of other activists had been a significant figure in lobbying for government funding for its establishment. Although managed by TAFE NSW, it was funded by the Commonwealth Government and set up as a cross-provider service to support adult literacy services in the whole range of the state's programs, including those developed by the NSW Adult Migrant Education Service, the Board of Adult Education and the Department of Corrective Services, as well as other small community-based providers. This was the same coalition of actors that came together to form the NSW Adult Literacy Council two years earlier. This time they came together to lobby for funding for ALIO. This relationship between TAFE and other providers later became a point of tension within the management of ALIO, but in reflecting on the early years, Kath White referred to the 'collegiality amongst providers from a lot of different statutory bodies or organisations. Really ideal conditions for getting something started' (Johnston, Kelly & Johnston 2001, p. 16).

The early days of ALIO were emblematic of the field in general. It was housed in a building in Redfern, a socially depressed inner-city suburb. White believed that 'it should be in a down-market rather than up-market area' (Johnston, Kelly & Johnston 2001, p. 10). This mirrored the physical location of many of the programs in these early days. In the immediate post-Kangan era, TAFE systems were experiencing considerable expansion and competition for facilities, so that in many colleges, ABE and other access programs were located in un-prepossessing, off-campus rented cottages. In general, these suited the adult literacy field of the time well, as many practitioners argued that ABE students would feel more comfortable in such surroundings, away from the main institutional buildings, echoing Richardson's injunction that 'an effective literacy program will almost certainly have to be conducted outside the formal institutional framework' (Richardson 1975, p. 96).

ALIO became a central gathering point for teachers, volunteer tutors and students. There are frequent references to the warm, welcoming atmosphere that was created, with the focus in these early years on volunteers. The teachers I spoke to confirmed ALIO's role as a highly valued part of the field. It was considered to be 'a hub of the literacy field, the physical and cultural centre, the meeting place' (Johnston, Kelly & Johnston 2001, p. 15).

It became a melting pot for ideas and a focus for the developing body of professional practice knowledge. The archive of ALIO's publications details the workshops that were held regularly with sessions delivered by local practitioners or visiting academics such as the Canadian Frank Smith, Americans Ken and Yetta Goodman and

Australian Brian Cambourne. When asked about the influences on their practice, many respondents mentioned these professional development sessions at ALIO.

Sharing examples of practical pedagogy became one of the central functions of ALIO, particularly in the early, formative years for the field. The British publications from the BBC campaign of the 1970s were disseminated through ALIO, as were a number of its own publications. The importance of these publications in informing their practice was recognised by many interviewees.

The community of practice

One of the striking and recurrent themes from my interviews with practitioners who were employed in these early years related to the vibrant and creative community of practice that emerged (Osmond 2016). It is perhaps one of the defining aspects of the field in this era and emerged as a key actor in the development of the professional discourse. Within a very short time, that community of practice had developed a relatively coherent body of professional practice knowledge, in spite of the fact that there was little research and published literature specific to the field (Lee & Wickert 1994; McCormack 2009).

White (1983) wrote of the early diversity of opinions concerning *pedagogy* that teachers brought with them and held to firmly, prompting disagreements such as that over the place of phonics or the advisability of individual versus small group tuition. However, she also found that teachers held to an almost universal body of incontrovertible educational *principles* that had come to define the professional practice knowledge of the field, and that I refer to above as The Adult Literacy Discourse. In spite of the differences of opinion on matters of practical pedagogy, she wrote that it was nevertheless possible to establish 'some common ground on which we all stood, the principles from which we felt all our practice should flow. It seemed possible to do this because, despite the above differences, there was an even stronger unanimity binding us' (p. 118).

This distinct body of professional practice knowledge is evident in the archival documents and is reflected in the reflections of my interviewees.

> I still have a wonderful sense of the energy and camaraderie that was around in, I guess, the 80s and very early 90s as adult literacy just burgeoned as a movement and you had a sense that you were building this fantastic, useful, powerful, (sorry, I'm getting a bit carried away) ... It was fantastic. (Anne – interview)

> And we were learning all the time. We were learning new stuff. Working in this common thing, and learning stuff together, feeling part of something that was a good thing to be doing. (Jan – interview)

The interviews also serve to highlight the ways in which that body of knowledge came into being. They refer to the rich mix of influences that practitioners brought to the field: influences that represent other threads of the actor network. They drew from their formal tertiary studies in associated disciplines, from professional development workshops and from the informal influence of colleagues (Osmond 2018). Many of the interviewees spoke of the access to an abundant array of journals, newsletters and books that characterised the 1980s and 1990s. When asked about her sense of a community of practice, Shirley mentioned some of these influences:

> You were getting together every term for a get-together, so you were building bonds, and you were turning up to professional developments with the same people so you knew who people were, you knew their stories, you knew what people were teaching, you learnt from them, you shared resources, you shared ideas, you had a sense that we were all doing a similar set of things and you belonged to a very big movement and on top of that you had journals tying you together so you were reading articles that some of us had written. A lot of people had done the same qualification, so you had that in common and we were run centrally in those days, so you did have a very strong sense of something that was state-wide. (Interview)

Collaboration

All of the interviewees spoke warmly of the spirit of sharing in those early years. Ideas and resources were readily shared around.

> We had meetings and talked about good ideas that worked and no one seemed to be 'this is mine'. I think we were very generous, and we were accepting as well' (Judith – interview).

A number of the interviewees who had worked in the south-west area of Sydney reflected on the fact that the teachers in that region developed an active informal professional development circle, 'absolutely organised by and from the grass roots; [we] got together on

Saturday' (Anne – interview). This was a cross-provider informal network, in the days before competition between providers rendered this not possible.

Kath White spoke of this collegiality as 'the great inspiring thing that gave us all energy' and referred to the outcome of this collaboration as 'generative'.

> Another word that I used then and still feel it is a very important word is generative – things generating – interaction between colleagues generates new ideas. (Interview)

Professional development

Professional development opportunities were plentiful in this early era of investment in education. The 'learning stuff together' that Jan referred to was facilitated in a large way by ALIO and the workshops and seminars that were held regularly there. ACAL and its affiliated state councils also ran well-supported annual conferences and occasional workshops.

The ability for people to get together was one of the factors that contributed to the strength of this community of practice in the view of many of the interviewees, even in the sparsely populated state of NSW. Rose, who was working in a regional area at the time, remembered a sense of a state-wide community of practice,

> because there was lots of money for professional development at the time. We went to conferences, workshops, came down here [to Sydney] for things… there was money for us to attend things around the regions as well. (Interview)

Searching for saliences

A number of the interviewees however also spoke of influences on their practice coming from their own moral judgement, or what Higgs et al. describe as 'personal knowledge about oneself as a person and in relationship with others' (cited in Kemmis 2005, p. 7), and Kemmis (2005) refers to as 'searching for saliences'.

When asked how she initially knew what to do with a new student or group of students, Kath White related her experience of setting up the first individual Learning Centre in TAFE in 1975, prior to the development of the adult literacy field and her exposure to the ideas coming out of the UK. She had planned a curriculum as she explained above, but 'as soon as I started to use it with real students, I knew it didn't work', so she developed a needs-based, individualised program for each student.

Judith related a similar experience from her pre-adult literacy employment, teaching a group of fire brigade employees who were being given some extra tuition to help them pass their exams for promotion.

> And I am stuck in this terrible situation – I don't actually know what to do, except naively I had some gut feelings so I set it up as ... individual programs for each student ....I did stuff that I didn't even know was part of literacy [teaching]. I'd have them tell me something and I'd write it down and then I'd get them to read it back. I'd never seen that, but it just seemed to be like a sensible thing to do because it would be their words. (Interview)

These teachers were drawing on their life-experiences reflexively in order to address particular practical problems. Many of the interviewees expressed something similar when asked about the influences they drew on to solve particular pedagogical problems.

> I think that was part of the beauty of adult literacy; that you responded to your students. And you filled in the forms and followed the curriculum or whatever but essentially you just kept doing what you thought your students needed. (Jan – interview)

Agency

Underpinning this community of practice was the sense of agency that the early practitioners spoke of and that Kath White had experienced from the very conception of the TAFE program. Several other participants reflected nostalgically on the fact that they had the ability to create the field as they went: the 'learning stuff together' and 'doing what you thought your students needed'.

Practitioners' sense of professional agency over their practice extended to the political sphere also. The establishment of ALIO did not originate with a government initiative but an initiative of a coalition of early NSW adult literacy pioneers. Kath White and Geoff Falkenmire had both visited the Adult Literacy Resource Agency (ALRA) in UK and envisaged something similar in NSW. White spoke of meeting with a group of advocates in the office of Alan

Cadman (MP), who she referred to as 'a good friend of adult literacy' in Australia and who helped write the application. Nationally also, there was a sense in which the profession had agency over the direction of its development through the influence of ACAL whose advice was actively sought by the federal government during this period (Zimmerman & Norton 1990).

This genteel advocacy became more strident lobbying in later years, when the need arose, as a number of interviewees reflected. Perhaps the first significant instance of the difficulties arising from this new field being accommodated within TAFE's bureaucracy arose over the matter of the TAFE enrolment form in 1982. Advocates had previously managed to argue successfully that, owing to privacy and confidentiality concerns, ABE students would be identified on the enrolment form by initials and date of birth only. Hilary recalls a new directive in 1982 that required adult basic education students to complete a normal TAFE enrolment form.

> [and I thought] 'No, our students aren't going to do that, their privacy is most important to many of them' ... so I thought, 'nup, nup, not having that', so I made myself an appointment with [the appropriate assistant director of TAFE] and took myself in to see him, and put the case for privacy for our students. [He said] 'Yeah, yeah, I can see your point, yeah, sounds sensible to me. You mean they would just put in their initials but not their addresses or personal details?' ... So he called out to someone to say, 'Just organise this for us will you so that those who are in the volunteer adult literacy program don't have to fill out the TAFE enrolment form'. (Interview)

In the late 1980s the tension was again over enrolment procedures and the proposed reintroduction of an administrative fee for all TAFE students, including ABE students. TAFE fees had been abolished in 1974, but by the late 1980s financial stringency was evident in TAFE.

> I can remember a couple of times in the late 1980s when the Greiner/Metherell government came in and they wanted to introduce fees. That really got the council going ... someone doing posters, someone writing to MPs ... and we won that. (Sam – interview)

That issue was revisited in 2003 and again in 2015, that final time with a different outcome.

National Policy on Languages

The late 1980s marked a high point in the development of the field of adult basic education in Australia with the 1987 implementation of the *National Policy on Languages* (NPL) (Lo Bianco 1987), heralding a three year initiative known as *the Adult Literacy Action Campaign*. The NPL was to become, in many ways, emblematic of what has been called 'Australia's literacy decade'(McKenna & Fitzpatrick 2004, p. 66), and enjoyed a significant international reputation in the field of language policy (Brock 2001). It is therefore an appropriate point to conclude this chapter, illustrating as it does many of the defining characteristics of this foundation era, including the agency experienced by adult literacy activists and practitioners to shape the policy discourse.

From early in the 1980s a coalition of multicultural and language education advocates had begun to lobby government for a national language policy, with the Hawke government finally inviting Professor Joseph Lo Bianco to develop such a policy. This is another instance of a coalition of actors with similar, though not identical, goals and motives coalescing to form a powerful actor network. Thus, the actor network responsible for delivering ABE's first key public policy document was not a network of ABE activists, but primarily multicultural and language education activists. Although Lo Bianco's background was language education and multiculturalism, he was another 'good friend of ABE' and his insistence on inclusion of adult literacy in the NPL was used as a crucial strategy in the efforts to secure funding for the field. The policy proposed that 'a concerted and well-planned campaign be implemented during 1988 to attempt to improve levels of adult literacy' (Lo Bianco 1987, p. 15), and recommended that '$5m be made available in 1987/88 for this campaign which is to be implemented on the expert advice and guidance of adult literacy groups' (p. 20).

This became the two-year *Adult Literacy Action Campaign* (ALAC), with funding of nearly $2m allocated per year. Most of this was to go to the states, but a significant amount was set aside for 'projects of national strategic significance' (Wickert 2001a, p. 79). Acting on the recommendation that the campaign should 'be implemented on the expert advice and guidance of adult literacy groups', the advice of ACAL was sought to decide on and to frame many of the resulting 'projects of national strategic significance' (Wickert 2001b). The state literacy councils were also invited to discussions about how their state's share of the money could most effectively be used. This was significant, and the evidence suggests that it was perhaps the last occasion on which the views of practitioners and academics in the field had been directly sought in the *framing* of policy. The archival data points to the frequent communication that had occurred between the government and literacy activists leading up to this time. For example, Rosie Wickert wrote in her President's report to the NSWALC in 1989 of the letters that the council had written to State and Commonwealth politicians:

> Replies were received to these letters and as a result, the Minister for Education's policy advisor met with us and listened to our concerns. The [ACAL] president has had ongoing contact with the Minister's office and we hope to be consulted when literacy issues arise. (Wickert 1989b, p. 1)

The practitioner network was still an important actor in shaping policy. However, by 1991, Wickert and Zimmerman were to write:

> These are heady days and they lay a heavy responsibility on our shoulders. This government initiative [ALAC] is the culmination of many years of lobbying, and since so little is known about the field, literacy practitioners have been given the go-ahead to make the recommendations about how the funds can best be used. I doubt that such an opportunity will present itself again. (1991, p. 184)

Indeed, such an opportunity did not present itself again.

Many of the projects funded under ALAC were aimed at extending provision and increasing the public profile of the field. However, significant amongst the 'projects of national strategic significance' were Wickert's survey of adult literacy, *No Single Measure* (1989a), and a study of the *Outcomes of Adult Literacy Programs* (Brennan, Clark & Dymock 1989), both projects that aimed at producing the much needed evidence on which to base requests for funding.

Wickert was an adult literacy academic and activist, and her survey *No Single Measure* adopted a definition of literacy as a social practice and advocated for a change to the notion that literacy is a discrete and quantifiable ability. The survey was based on a similar one in the USA by Kirsch and Jungeblut (1986), from which she took the title: 'There is no single measure or specific point on a scale that separates the "literate" from the "illiterate"' (Wickert 1989a, p. title page). This was a more sophisticated approach than that adopted in previous surveys (for example, Goyen 1977). It also aimed to gather information about the survey subjects' literacy activities in order to explore whether people's attitudes to literacy activities are related to their performance (Wickert 1989a).

Another significant project funded under ALAC explored the *Outcomes of Adult Literacy Programs* (Brennan, Clark & Dymock 1989). Importantly, it focused on outcomes from the point of view of the learners, a methodology that replicated an earlier study by Charnley and Jones (1979) in the UK. The study concluded that 'for governments, there is reassurance that their funds have been well spent, because from the perspective of the adult learners there have been positive outcomes in economic and social, as well as personal terms' (Brennan 1990, p. 51).

It is not likely, however, that the government would have taken much reassurance from this study in a political context that was in rapid change, a context in which focus on outcomes from the student perspective carried little weight as I will discuss in the next chapter.

NSW's share of this Commonwealth money funded such projects as a series of videos to teach literacy/numeracy and basic vocational skills to hard-to-reach and isolated groups such as prisoners, rural and Aboriginal students, and other projects to target other, previously neglected sectors of the community. For example a program targeted migrant women to enable them 'to develop their reading and writing skills in order to have greater access to community resources and institutions ... [and to] fulfil personal writing needs in English and to develop confidence and self-esteem' (Persson 1988, p. 4).

Such programs with personal objectives, expressed in humanist language, were unlikely to attract Commonwealth attention or funding in the coming decades. This period, following the release of the *National Policy on Languages*, marked perhaps the end of the period in which adult literacy was conceived in both professional and policy discourse as having objectives conducive to both social justice and human capital ends. Such language progressively dropped out of the policy discourse for the remainder of the narrative.

Discussion and conclusion

This chapter has traced the development of the field in NSW from the small number of programs operating on an ad hoc basis in the mid-1970s to a system of provision in the late 1980s that was professionalised and extensive. The welfare image of the field had been left behind and it was now a credible, professional field. The coalition of non-human actors that had created a context against which the field

The foundation years 57

developed was joined in this era by a number of human actors and coalitions of human actors. Given the socially and culturally liberal milieu of the time, they experienced an agency in their ability to help shape the discourse, that is foreign to present practitioners, and which was to fade with the end of this era. However, for perhaps this first decade, they were powerful actors in shaping this project of social ordering. Some were individual actors, and some were coalitions of actors such as those individuals from similar fields who came together to form the initial state peak body (NSWALC) and to lobby governments for additional services and for the introduction of a national policy. Most, however, exercised their agency through the vibrant and creative community of practice that was a distinctive feature of this era. It developed an almost universally agreed on body of professional practice knowledge and a set of widely adhered to underpinning principles based on a humanist discourse of student-centredness, a discourse that I have referred to as **The Adult Literacy Discourse**.

Importantly, this humanist discourse was not only represented in the professional discourse but reflected much of the public discourse also. These were ideas centred on the importance of helping to create a world based on social justice and the holistic development of individuals, as reflected in the few government and institutional policies of the time. Ade-Ojo and Duckworth (2015), in reference to this period in the UK, refer to 'a range of events and factors within the society [which] stood in place of conventional policy' (p. 31) at a time before the government became more closely involved with the field. A parallel reading of the field in Australia would also serve to highlight the important role of the actors referred to in this era, that were standing 'in place of conventional policy' which was to emerge towards the end of the 1980s.

References

Ade-Ojo, G. & Duckworth, V. 2015, *Adult literacy policy and practice: From intrinsic values to instrumentalism*, Palgrave Macmillan, Hampshire, UK.
Bee, B. 1990, 'Teaching to empower: Women and literacy', *Australian Journal of Reading* 13(1), 53–59.
Black, S. 2018, 'From "empowerment" to "compliance": Neoliberalism and adult literacy provision in Australia', *Journal for Critical Education Policy Studies* 16(1), 104–144.
Black, S. & Bee, B. 2018, 'Adult literacy and liberal-progressive pedagogy: Australian contexts', *Research in Post-Compulsory Education* 23(2), 181–201.
Brennan, B. 1990, 'Outcomes of literacy programs: Learners' perspectives', *Open Letter* 1(1), 47–52.

Brennan, B., Clark, R. & Dymock, D. 1989, *Outcomes of adult literacy programs*, Department of Employment, Education and Training, Canberra.

Brock, P. 2001, 'Australia's language', in J. Lo Bianco & R. Wickert (eds), *Australian policy activism in language and literacy*, Language Australia, Melbourne, pp. 49–76.

Callon, M. 1986, 'Some elements of a sociology of translation: Domestication of the scallops and the fishermen of St Brieuc Bay', in J. Law (ed.), *Power, action and belief: A new sociology of knowledge?* Routledge and Kegan Paul, London.

Campbell, B. 2009, *Reading the fine print – A history of the Victorian Adult Literacy and Basic Education Council (VALBEC) 1978–2008*, Victorian Adult Literacy and Basic Education Council, Springvale South.

Charnley, A. & Jones, H. 1979, *The concept of success in adult literacy*, Adult Literacy and Basic Skills Unit, London.

Duckworth, V. & Ade-Ojo, G. 2016, 'Journey through transformation: A case study of two literacy learners', *Journal of Transformative Education* 14(4), 285–304.

Freire, P. 1972, *Pedagogy of the oppressed*, Penguin, Middlesex, England.

Freire, P. & Macedo, D. 1987, *Literacy: Reading the word and the world*, Routledge and Kegan Paul, London.

Goozee, G. 2001, *The development of TAFE in Australia*, NCVER, Adelaide.

Goyen, J. 1977, *Adult illiteracy in Sydney*, Australian Association of Adult Education, Canberra.

Hamilton, M. & Hillier, Y. 2006, *Changing faces of adult literacy, language and numeracy: A critical history*, Trentham Books, Stoke on Trent.

Hammond, J. & Wickert, R. 1993, 'Pedagogical relations between adult ESL and adult literacy: Some directions for research', *Open Letter* 3(2), 16–31.

Hazell, P. 1998, *Student outcomes: Investigating competency-based curriculum in adult basic education*, University of Technology, Sydney.

Holt, J. 1976, *Instead of education*, Penguin, New York.

Illich, I. 1973, *Deschooling society*, Penguin, Harmondsworth.

Johnston, B., Kelly, S. & Johnston, K. 2001, *The rise and fall of the NSW Adult Literacy and Information Office*, NSW ALNARC, Sydney.

Jones, H. & Charnley, A. 1978, *Adult literacy: A study of its impact*, NIAE, London.

Jurmo, P. 1989, 'History in the making: Key players in the creation of participatory alternatives', in A. Fingeret & P. Jurmo (eds), *Participatory literacy education*, Jossey-Bass, San Francisco, pp. 73–80.

Kangan, M.C. 1974, *TAFE in Australia: Report on needs in technical and further education*, AGPS, Canberra.

Kebby, H. 1989, 'The Certificate in Basic Education', *Good Practice in Australian Adult Literacy and Basic Education* 4, 15.

Kemmis, S. 2005, 'Is mathematics education a practice? Mathematics teaching?', in M. Goos, C. Kaynes & R. Brown (eds), *Fourth International Mathematics Education and Society Conference*, Griffith University, Gold Coast, Qld, pp. 19–38.

Kirsch, I. & Jungeblut, A. 1986, *Literacy: Profiles of America's young adults*, National Assessment of Educational Progress, Princeton, NJ.
Knowles, M. 1990, *The adult learner: A neglected species*, Gulf, Houston.
Lee, A. & Wickert, R. 1994, 'Deconstructing adult literacy teaching', *Open Letter* 5(1), 55–68.
Lo Bianco, J. 1987, *National policy on languages*, Commonwealth Department of Education, Canberra, ACT.
McCormack, R. 2009, 'Groping towards our field', *Fine Print* 32(3), 9–11.
McGuirk, J. 1998, 'Tracking writing through 49 issues of *Literacy Broadsheet*', *Literacy Broadsheet* (50), 19–25.
McKenna, R. & Fitzpatrick, L. 2004, *Building sustainable adult literacy provision: A review of international trends in adult literacy policy and programs – Support document*, NCVER, Adelaide, Australia.
Merriam, S. & Brockett, R. 2007, *The profession and practice of adult education: An introduction*, Jossey-Bass, San Francisco.
Neill, A.S. 1968, *Summerhill*, Pelican, Middlesex.
Nelson, A. 1985, *'The community development approach to literacy'*, paper presented to the Adult Literacy and Community Development Workshop, August 19–25, Armidale.
Nelson, A. 1997, 'Arch Nelson reminisces about adult literacy', in P. Ward & R. Wickert (eds), *Towards a history of adult literacy in Australia: A record of the history of adult literacy weekend*, Language Australia, Belconnen, ACT, pp. 12–19.
Nelson, A. 2010, 'Recollections on the Association over five decades', *Australian Journal of Adult Learning* 50(3), 529–534.
Nelson, A. & Dymock, D. 1986, *Adult literacy and community development: Report of a workshop held at the University of New England*, University of New England, Armidale.
NSW Adult Literacy Council1987, *The use of volunteers in TAFE adult literacy programs*, unpublished report.
Osmond, P. 2016, 'What happened to our community of practice? The early development of adult basic education in NSW through the lens of professional practice theory', *Literacy and Numeracy Studies* 24(2), 3–25.
Osmond, P. 2018, 'Adult basic education in NSW 1970–2018: Official stories and stories from practice', MEd thesis, University of Technology Sydney.
Papen, U. 2005, *Adult literacy as social practice*, Routledge, London.
Persson, M. 1988, 'ACAL news', *Literacy Exchange* 4.
Richardson, E.C. 1975, *TAFE in Australia: Second report on needs in technical and further education*, AGPS, Canberra.
Sanguinetti, J. 1992, 'Teaching with Freire in Australia: Some questions and lessons', *Open Letter* 3(1), 39–46.
Searle, J. 1999, 'An unsung band of heroes: A history of adult literacy in Queensland 1970–1995', PhD thesis, Griffith University, Queensland.
Searle, J. 2000, *'To be or not to be? Is there a future for adult literacy?'*, paper presented to the ACAL, Perth.

Shipway, A. (ed.) *1988–1991, Good practice in Australian adult literacy and basic education*, ALAC, Tasmania.

Street, B. 1995, *Adult literacy in the United Kingdom – A history of research and practice*, National Centre on Adult Literacy, Philadelphia.

Tusting, K. 2009, '"I am not a 'good' teacher, I don't do all their paperwork": teacher resistance to accountability demands in the English Skills for Life strategy', *Literacy and Numeracy Studies* 17(3), 6–26.

White, K. 1978, *Voluntarism and bureaucracy: Trends in the utilisation of volunteers in adult literacy programmes in New South Wales*, University of New England, Armidale.

White, K. 1983, 'Conflict, principles and practice in adult literacy', *Australian Journal of Reading* 6(3), 117–127.

White, K. & Gribble, H. 1986, 'Gift work defined', *Literacy Exchange, Journal of NSWALC* (August), 43–52.

Whitelock, D. 1974, *The great tradition: A history of adult education in Australia*, University of Queensland Press, Brisbane.

Wickert, R. 1989a, *No single measure*, Commonwealth Dept. Employment, Education and Training, Canberra.

Wickert, R. 1989b, 'President's Report', *Literacy Exchange* 1, 1.

Wickert, R. 2001a, 'Politics, activism and processes of policy production: Adult literacy in Australia', in J. Lo Bianco & R. Wickert (eds), *Australian policy activism in language and literacy*, Language Australia, Melbourne, pp. 77–93.

Wickert, R. 2001b, 'Processes, politics and the effects of policy text production', in J. Lo Bianco & R. Wickert (eds), *Australian policy activism in language and literacy*, Language Australia, Melbourne.

Wickert, R. & Zimmerman, J. 1991, 'Adult basic education in Australia: Questions of integrity', in M. Tennant (ed.), *Adult and continuing education in Australia: Issues and practices*, Routledge, London, pp. 175–206.

Zimmerman, J. & Norton, M. 1990, 'The challenges for adult literacy in Australia', in J. D'Cruz & P. Langford (eds), *Issues in Australian education*, Longman Cheshire, Melbourne, pp. 144–168.

4 A new discourse emerges

Introduction

From the early 1990s public and policy discussions around literacy increasingly became centred on the theme of vocational training and human resource investment, discussions that have continued to the time of writing. Adult basic education (ABE) became subsumed under the umbrella of Vocational Education and Training (VET), with its increased marketisation of provision, resulting in a substantial shift from public sector to private sector provision as the march of neoliberalist ideology took firm control of policy on both sides of the traditional political spectrum. The policy settings of the 1990s created by this context were to provide the direction for the development of the field to the present time. Those challenging this inexorable shift in the value attributed to literacy no longer held a powerful position in the actor network shaping the field; a new and powerful coalition of actors had replaced them.

Since the late 1990s there have been repeated professional discussions about the future of the field in this less accommodating socio-economic climate. The theme of 'at the crossroads' became a constant and ongoing refrain. For example, in 1999 Kell wrote that 'Literacy and language policy in Australia is at a crossroads where market ideology and the pragmatics of provision are on a metaphoric collision course' (1999, p. 2).

It is ironic that the beginning of the period covered by this chapter, the period from the late 1980s to the late 1990s, has been referred to as 'Australia's literacy decade' (McKenna & Fitzpatrick 2004, p. 66). This was the period in which Australia gained global recognition as a world leader and innovator in adult basic education policy and provision (NALA 2011). Australian adult literacy had come into the mainstream; however, this was to come at a cost in the minds of many practitioners. The government's neoliberal faith in the effectiveness of market forces enabled powerful industry-based lobby groups to intervene to influence policy outcomes. The education lobby group, and, in particular, the *adult* education lobby, is not one with a powerful voice and in the new millennium that voice was ignored.

The field was to become increasingly under government influence and control so that by the end of this period, many felt that they had lost control of the professional agenda. Whilst the early programs discussed in the last chapter had aimed to provide informal, student-centred, needs-based provision, informed by ideals of humanist education, the period since the mid-1980s saw a shift to a new discourse: one that was characterised by economic efficiency, corporate managerialism and competition. Neoliberalism was becoming the dominant economic discourse.

This is a seminal period in the ABE narrative. An understanding of the national and international socio-political developments of this era and the actors responsible for promoting them is particularly significant in understanding the contexts of ABE provision and the discourses that have surrounded them for the ensuing decades.

The new coalition of actors on the global stage

The seeds of radical change that the field was to experience in the coming decades had been sown as early as the late 1970s and had diverse roots. In the global sphere, 1974–1975 saw the collapse of the stock market with the resulting collapse of the principles of Keynesian economic management, principles that had supported the emergence of public programs such as the early adult literacy programs. Thus, the seeds of economic collapse were being sown even as the fledgling programs were emerging. Harvey has argued that 'future historians may well look upon the years 1978–80 as a revolutionary turning-point in the world's social and economic history' (2005, p. 10), with the socially brutal responses of the Thatcher and Reagan governments to their worsening economies. This chapter will argue that these years had certainly produced conditions which presaged a revolutionary turning point in the field of ABE in Australia and beyond.

Market liberal economics

President Ronald Reagan's words at his inauguration in 1980 were emblematic of the global transformation of socio-economic policy: 'In this period, government is not the solution, it is the problem ... It is time to check and reverse the growth of government' (cited in

Marginson 1997, p. 76). In this climate of economic crisis, the Keynesian economics that had supported big government gave way to a market liberal position whose best known exponents are perhaps Milton Friedman in the USA and the influential Austrian political economist F.A. Hayek. Both Friedman and Hayek visited Australia on extensive speaking tours between 1975 and 1981. For them and their fellow market liberals, any investment in non-market-based programs that were not productive of wealth was seen to be damaging to the economy, a position that came to be known as neoliberalism. Although the term is frequently dismissed as something of an 'intellectual swear word' (Mirowski & Plehwe 2015, p. 35), it is possible to identify some common threads of its meaning in contemporary usage. At its core, it was a monetarist policy promoting the protection of free markets as a defence against the spread of socialism and communism: the unwelcome and deeply feared ideologies that appeared to be spreading at the close of the First World War. Its message was a simple one: the superiority of the market over all forms of government intervention. Although it has its origins as a monetarist policy, it is more easily understood as an ideology, one based on a redefined role for government in the promotion of the free market (Stedman Jones 2012).

The ways in which the ideas of these market liberals became the global hegemony of neoliberalism further illuminates the actor network that I trace in this book. The power of the neoliberal ideology is attributed to a shadowy but deliberate global network of influences or 'thought collectives'. These are described as 'communit[ies] of persons mutually exchanging ideas or maintaining intellectual interaction' (L. Fleck, cited in Mirowski & Plehwe 2015, p. 626). This exchange of ideas was to be done through the establishment of think tanks with the generous support of corporate sponsors; by the popularisation of these ideas by journalists and politicians; and by the lobbying activities of influential business entities who had felt their interests were threatened by the state intervention of the Keynesian era.

A number of these think tanks in Australia bear titles that are now household names and their links to the actor network that now surrounds the field of ABE are easy to trace. Goodall (2019) links the names of well-known influential Australian business people, politicians and media moguls, to Australian neoliberal think tanks that have connection to both Hayek and Friedman. For example, David Kemp, who we will meet again later in this chapter as minister for education in the Howard conservative government, features amongst those who gathered around the master neoliberals and the think tanks that they engendered or influenced as early as the mid-1970s.

The New Right

The global influence of market liberal economics was accompanied by the ascendency of the political New Right: 'a political movement uniting market liberals and mainstream political conservatives' (Marginson 1997, p. 78). The monetarist policies of the early neoliberals served as something of a Trojan horse to promote a range of other allied policies related to the reconfigured role of government and the public service. The neoliberal policies of competition and cost effectiveness brought with them the privatisation of essential social services, the influence of corporate managerialism, and a proliferation of audit devices under the banner of accountability. More importantly, the growth in the unequal distribution of resources was seen as an inevitable characteristic of the ideal market system (Mirowski 2015).

The influence of the global New Right in succeeding decades in all OECD countries is not surprising, given that it had bipartisan support from both sides of politics, including in Australia from both Labor and conservative politicians. Australia in the 1970s had seen growing bipartisan support for this ultimate reversal of the growth of the public sector, thus setting the scene for the policy settings that were to emerge in the 1980s.

The human capital ideology and the OECD

Chapter 2 referred to the central role that UNESCO had played globally in promoting the human rights discourse of the post-war years. However, policy makers had already begun to feel that the pursuit of access and equity had failed to bring about the promised social redistribution so that by the second half of the 1970s there was a worldwide shift to remove equality of opportunity from policy discourse. The UN and its affiliated transnational organisations had been ready targets for neoliberal ideology (Bair 2015) and by the late 1980s restructures and internal tensions in UNESCO had sidelined its ABE focus and its social justice discourse thus making way for the human capital discourse of the OECD as a policy driver on the international stage (Limage 2009). By the mid-1980s the OECD 'called for the abandonment of the more far-reaching equality objectives of the 1960s ... Social redistribution through education was too difficult a project, and should be abandoned' (Marginson 1997, p. 195). Over successive years, the Labor Party began to distance itself from Whitlam's 1972 claim that 'education should be seen as the great instrument for the promotion of equality' (Marginson 1997, p. 46) with declining emphasis on equality of opportunity as a driver of its policies. Thus, by the time that adult literacy began to enter the public discourse in Australia and programs began to materialise in the late 1970s, the rhetoric of access and equity had already begun to disappear from the global political discourse.

The shift in discourse was, however, largely hastened by economic considerations. From the late 1980s it started to become clear to the governments of Western economies that those economies that were well endowed with natural resources were not necessarily the richest or most competitive. The fact that countries such as Japan, Singapore and Switzerland had few natural resources but were economically successful posed a paradox to the orthodoxy of the economic advantages of natural resources. The way forward was obviously to garner human capital (Lo Bianco 1999).

The pressures to re-define the literacy discourse were felt in similar democracies such as the UK and USA. With the UK's entrance to the European Union, the Manpower Services Commission's access to considerable funding became a new and important factor driving the narrative (Hamilton & Hillier 2006). The literacy skills that became prized were autonomous, transferrable and measurable 'basic' skills that, it was believed, individuals needed to acquire to be competitive in the workplace. The direct influence of these developments on the Australian context can be seen for example in the 'series of pilgrimages' of bureaucrats from Australia's Hawke Labor government to fellow bureaucrats of the UK Manpower Services Commission during the Thatcher era (Ryan 2011, p. 9).

The OECD and a new *immutable mobile*

Whilst UNESCO had been a key actor in the field of ABE in its foundation years, the OECD began to take its place. The discourse of social justice in adult education began to be displaced by a focus on the relationship between vocational education and economic productivity.

This shift was fuelled by a series of international research reports during the 1990s, demonstrating for many nations (including the UK, USA and Australia) apparent inadequate literacy skills in comparison to other similar nations. The first International Adult Literacy Survey (IALS) was organised by the OECD between 1994 and 1998 in order to provide comparisons of literacy levels between countries, and to further cement a connection between literacy and the need to improve economic productivity. Further iterations of IALS followed, including the most recent, the Programme for the International Assessment of Adult Competencies (PIAAC). These surveys aimed to reflect the multiplicity of skills used by adults in an advanced industrialised country.

It has been argued, however, that they did not reflect this multiplicity of skills, and were based on a view of literacy as an autonomous, context-free information-processing set of cognitive skills (Hamilton & Barton 2000) with data collected on responses to a particular kind of text only (St Clair 2012). Although these tests have been the subject of such serious methodological critique, and critique of the ways in which they have been used (St Clair 2012), they have remained a powerful actor shaping policy discussions.

The view of literacy promoted in the tests was reflected in domestic debate concerning allocation of government funds. These surveys have 'framed the terms of the debate, [and] defined the scope and content of "literacy need"'(Hamilton, Macrae & Tett 2001, p. 23). The literature demonstrates the ways in which these OECD surveys became the new *immutable mobiles* (Latour 1987), adding authority to the message of a literacy crisis threatening national productivity (Black & Yasukawa 2016; Hamilton 2017; Hamilton & Barton 2000; Yasukawa & Black 2016; Yasukawa, Hamilton & Evans 2017). These surveys had replaced the humanist message of UNESCO's *Learning to be* (Faure 1972) as an *immutable mobile* in public and policy discourse.

The media and the new immutable mobile

The media also played a part in promoting the instrumentalist and employment-related view of literacy, mainly through its interpretation and promulgation of the results of the OECD's international literacy surveys. In 2000 the OECD published a report titled *Literacy in the Information Age* (OECD 2000) which highlighted the link between literacy, earnings and wage differentials but also provided a range of nuanced and complex data related to literacy for social outcomes. As well as relating gains in literacy levels to 'the effective functioning of labour markets and for the economic success and social advancement of both individuals and societies' (p. iii), the report also pointed to implications for literacy and life-long learning:

> Literacy skills are maintained and strengthened through regular use. While schooling provides an essential foundation, the evidence suggests that only through informal learning and the active use of literacy skills in daily activities – both at home and at work – will higher levels of proficiency be attained. (OECD 2000, p. xiv)

In Australia, these concepts of informal and life-long learning had been embraced in earlier decades as demonstrated by the previous chapter and continued to be embraced in the professional discourse. But they were not taken up by the media and did not make their way into the public discourse. The introduction to the report suggested that the data 'offer policy makers a useful tool for policy analysis and for crafting policies and programmes that can contribute to economic and social progress' (p. iii). However, in Australia, as in other similar countries, the media focussed on a simplistic link between literacy and national productivity, further entrenching the human capital argument as it related to literacy. The wealth of data that related to public and civic participation, for example, remained un-examined in the public and policy sphere.

Results of the PIAAC survey, like the others before it, were met with a similar response from the media and pressure on policy makers. In Australia these unexamined 'facts' such as the following became the obligatory starting point for a raft of reports commissioned by the industry groups: 'Close to half of Australia's working-age population (44 per cent) has low literacy skills (level 1 and 2) as measured in the Adult Literacy and Life Skills Survey in 2006' (Skills Australia 2011, p. 25).

This statistic became ubiquitous in any media discussion of literacy, so that the public and policy discourse was tied to it.

A new coalition of Australian actors

The economic conditions that led to the ascendency of Keynesian economics had changed almost before the recommendations of the Kangan Committee (which had recommended the early adult literacy programs) could be enacted. The effects of a recession that had begun in Australia around 1974 were being keenly felt by the middle of the 1980s. Australia's manufacturing industry had continued to collapse, there was lingering unemployment, and Australia's status in international markets was declining. These were the conditions that prompted treasurer Keating to make his famous 'banana republic' speech in 1986, warning that, unless Australia urgently addressed reform of its industrial base, it risked becoming another 'banana republic', thus raising anxiety in the community concerning the health of the economy (Goozee 2001). The crash of the US stock market in 1987 added further urgency to the need for reform. There followed a range of changes to the basic policy settings affecting the field that were to have repercussions for decades to come. Business, government and unions were in agreement that change was needed in industrial work practices and that skill levels needed to be raised to world standards. The Vocational Education and Training (VET) sector was thus implicated in the need for reform and a new and powerful coalition of actors formed around the new project of social re-ordering of VET and ultimately of ABE.

This story of imminent economic crisis has remained a constant in the public imaginary, in spite of ample evidence that the Australian economy has continued to be remarkably healthy relative to other similar Western economies. Nevertheless, the media, government and industry groups have continued to make frequent references to the nation's precarious economic position, and the role that inadequate literacy skills plays in this.

Australian microeconomic reform and LLN

Unemployment was increasing steeply, a situation that brought into sharp focus those whose literacy skills were deemed to be the cause of their unemployment. As Street (1990) remarked, 'governments have a tendency to blame the victims at a time of high unemployment and "illiteracy" is one convenient way of shifting debate away from lack of jobs and onto people's own supposed lack of fitness for work' (p. 6).

Change was also apparent in the types of work opportunities available. A rapidly changing industrial base, the shrinking of jobs in the manufacturing industries and growth of jobs in the service industries all brought constant needs for reskilling, retraining and reorganisation of the workplace in the process of industrial award restructuring. For example, one of the industrial reforms recommended was the organisation of workforces into more flexible teams with devolved responsibility, thus increasing the need for communication at all levels and normalising multiskilling and devolution of many of the tasks that were once the prerogative of management.

A further crucial change came with the 1988 national wage case that connected wage gains and career progression to training and the gaining of qualifications. Workers whose literacy and numeracy skills had been adequate to the requirements of their jobs now found that they needed another set of literacy and numeracy skills to undertake the required accreditation for their jobs. There developed a growing awareness on the part of government and industry that many in the workforce did not have the literacy and numeracy skills to embark on this re-training; that the skills taught in school may not be appropriate for the modern workforce. Unions also shared this concern and in particular were keen to safeguard the interests of those on the bottom of the ladder and to optimise their training opportunities (Brown 2006; Gribble & Bottomley 1989). The new work order put great stress on the need for continual change and adaptation in a process of lifelong learning. This had implications for language, literacy and numeracy competencies of the workplace, and cemented the link with vocational training.

The link was made clear in the following bold statement made by the Secretary of the Australian Council of Trade Unions at a meeting with members of ACAL: 'Your time has come. The door of history has opened for you. Award restructure can't happen without you' (Gribble 1990, p. 41). With this seductive statement, an important *moment of translation* (Callon 1986) was occurring, with influential members of the ABE community of practice being *mobilised* and *enrolled* into the new project. The support of representatives of the union movement in this shift to the human capital discourse would have been particularly reassuring to those adult literacy activists and practitioners whose concern was for the well-being of working class and marginalised citizens. Having been co-opted into the cause of economic competitiveness and vocational training, literacy and numeracy provision was about to be shifted into the mainstream industrial training frameworks of the VET system. The issue of adult literacy had been *re-problematised* (Callon 1986) with its human capital value placed to the fore.

The changed role of systems of government

The changes to the VET system that are discussed in this chapter were just one outcome of a far-reaching transformation in the way that government conceived of its function. By 1988 the Australian government had signalled that its strategies of micro-economic reform would be applied to the systems of government also and the work of the public sector became dominated by the philosophies of the New Right (Marginson 1997; Yeatman 1993). It no longer saw itself as a public service-deliverer, and the role and identity of bureaucrats who had previously been responsible for such programs changed. The goals of portfolio advocacy that earlier bureaucrats brought to their roles were replaced by goals of economic efficiency, rendering them more impervious to lobbying by special interest groups (Yeatman 1993).

In spite of this imminent transformation, for a short period in the early 1990s the adult literacy policy field had benefited from a number of bureaucrats with strong portfolio expertise. They included a number of 'insider policy activists' (Brock 2001, p. 48) co-opted into the bureaucracy, and placed in positions to influence policy directions. They were academics and practitioners with a background in adult literacy or allied fields who helped to lay the policy framework for 'Australia's literacy decade' (McKenna & Fitzpatrick 2004, p. 66). However, they too soon became sidelined.

In her essay 'Political amnesia: how we forgot to govern' (2015), Tingle refers to the current rapid turn-over of public servants who had become generalists rather than portfolio advocates and who now had little institutional memory. She cites Ken Henry, Treasury Secretary of the Australian Government from 2001 to 2011, who warned that many government departments have 'lost the capacity to develop policy; but not just that, they have lost their memory. I seriously doubt there is any serious policy development going on in most government departments' (p. 13).

By the end of the 1990s, the role of the bureaucracy had become primarily one of economic management, employing the corporate management techniques and business practices applicable to economic production; 'government' had become 'governance' (Ball & Junemann 2018, p. 45). These were techniques such as centrally regulated program planning, product definition and measurement of outputs (Marginson 1997, p. 89), all overseen by stringent accountability and compliance protocols. These scientific management approaches, when applied to education, led to outcomes such as competency-based training and the bureaucratic categorisation of levels of literacy and numeracy skills in order to measure program outputs.

VET in Australia

In spite of the more straitened economic times, the Australian VET system had undergone remarkable expansion in the 1980s and 90s, due to considerable injection of Commonwealth funding, with the state-based public providers initially enjoying almost exclusive access to these funds. This period marked another era of expansion of VET provision almost on the scale of the late 1960s and early 1970s. However, in this period the objective was the development of those skills and talents needed for national economic competitiveness rather than the Keynesian notion of the broad development of skills and talents of the citizenry (Marginson 1997).

The Kangan report had introduced the concept of *education* into the previous *training* culture of the technical college system; however the gap between the training and education cultures had been widening

A new discourse emerges   71

since shortly after their marriage by Kangan. This gap gained extra impetus from the deteriorating economic climate. The pressure for VET policy to return to its earlier vocationalism was receiving increasing support.

Kaye Schofield (1994) refers to the 'clash of the titans': the training tribe and the education tribe. She describes it as a struggle between two competing world views, those represented by the liberalist education of the Kangan era, and those represented by the proponents of the new training reform agenda. In the process further education tended to drop off the agenda. As this chapter shows, as ABE became VET, education dropped off its agenda also.

Influence of industry

This period marked the beginning of increasing influence of industry in VET policy and the public discourse surrounding education and training. Industry bodies were *mobilised* and *enrolled* as actors in the new project: the re-invention of the VET system, and thus the re-invention of ABE.

Business interests clearly believed that they had a role in repositioning the VET sector. In 1986 a survey conducted by the Business Council of Australia found that:

> 88 per cent of its members believed business should be more vigorous in influencing 'educational objectives and practices', and 55 per cent thought standards would improve if business was more involved in educational decision making and management. (Sinclair 1986)

New advisory bodies sprang up, wielding strong influence on government policy making, as industry moved into a partnership role with government in the VET sphere. Thus, a powerful actor network consisting of government, industry and unions, with transnational agencies such as the OECD in the background, coalesced around the issue of adult literacy, as an integral part of the VET system.

These employer bodies, industry lobby groups and organisations had easy and direct access to government and to resources to fund research demonstrating the link between levels of literacy and economic prosperity (for example, Australian Industry Group 2012, 2015, 2016; Industry Skills Council 2011; Shomos 2010), research that was simply designed to legitimate its desired policy directions (Black & Yasukawa 2016).

72 *A new discourse emerges*

The National Training Reform Agenda (NTRA)

A major policy and discourse driver in this transition period was John Dawkins, the Labor minister for the new Commonwealth super portfolio of Employment, Education and Training. Dawkins was conscious of and sympathetic to the shift in OECD policy direction outlined above, since he had been active in the OECD (Ryan 2011). His department was staffed at the senior levels by 'economists who were mostly conservative and market liberal in outlook, and espoused key policy positions popularised by the New Right' (Marginson 1997, p. 152). His policies further formalised the integration of education with employment and training programs.

As a demonstration of the shift in priorities, Dawkins even insisted on a name change for his new department. He stated that,

> Following the 1987 Federal Election, I accepted my present portfolio on the understanding that its originally proposed name be rearranged so that the word 'employment' was placed first. I did this in order to emphasise that policies in education and training must be subordinate to the national economic imperative of achieving the optimal employment of our people. (Dawkins 1990, cited in Goozee 2001, p. 79)

Reforms to the VET sector came under the title of the National Training Reform Agenda (NTRA), a collection of government policies achieved through tripartite agreements of government, unions and industry. As Ryan (2011, p. 11) noted, 'this was effectively a replacement for the Kangan philosophy and programs'. As such, it represented a further key *moment* in the development of the field of ABE. A set of new advisory bodies was created; they became government's new industry partners, advising on policy formulation, and excluding training providers (at this time, almost exclusively the public training provider). There were three major NTRA reforms that were to impact ABE practice and provision: the introduction of a competency-based training system, and the associated competency-based assessment, and eventually the opening up of the training market to private providers.

Competency-Based Training (CBT)

The Commonwealth's enthusiasm for CBT began to build from about 1990, following the British example and encouraged by support from industry bodies such as the Business Council of Australia (BCA) and from the Australian Council of Trade Unions (ACTU) (Marginson 1997). A plethora of reports was commissioned, each in support of a competency-based system of training, with competencies defined as work related attributes, thus binding education and training to the expectations of industry. Unions were also enthusiastic supporters of CBT since they were keen to see the skills of their members recognised and to support their career progression, especially for those on the bottom of the career ladder (Brown 2006).

Since ABE was now tightly embedded in VET, its practitioners were to struggle with the inappropriate requirements of CBT on their practice for decades to come. Gonczi (2004) describes how, at the emergence of competency-based education, the proponents of the concept that guided Australia's NRTA had little real idea of what competency involved, so that 'what evolved was a highly reductionist and behaviourist concept of competence, based on the British model' (p. 20). These were the competencies that were easily observable and assessable so that the more affective and holistic outcomes that ABE practice had valued were sidelined (see also Angus et al. 2013; Hager 2004, 2016; Wheelahan 2016; Wheelahan & Moodie 2011).

The first connection that most NSW ABE teachers had with the *National Training Reform Agenda* was with NSW TAFE's *Certificate in Adult Foundation Education* (CAFE) which was accredited in 1995. By this time the requirement for it to be written in CBT brought a radical re-thinking of the concept of a basic education curriculum, and fundamental changes to course provision. The course developers were faced with the need to accommodate both the needs of ABE learners and the changed requirements for accreditation. In addition, for the first time, course developers were faced with the need to produce a product that could compete in the training market and be used to tender for Commonwealth-funded programs, given the requirement that tenders for these programs must be based on accredited, CBT-based curricula.

In an attempt to reconcile these requirements, the writers endeavoured to make explicit its theoretical underpinning. What resulted was a very large (six volume) and, to some, unwieldy course manual. Many teachers had mixed responses to the course with many taking a negative position based fundamentally on their opposition to the economic rationale of the training reform agenda. For many this conflict between the traditional philosophy of ABE provision and CBT in the new course was focussed in particular on the inability 'to meet the specific demands of all learners' (Hazell 1998, pp. 24–25).

74 A new discourse emerges

Most teachers at the time (and since) tried to accommodate the needs of the new context with traditional ABE principles and with what they believed to be the needs of the students in their classes.

> I think teachers had to find their way through, because they had to still cling to the importance of taking learners' goals and so forth, and valuing individuals. (Shirley – interview)

This issue of larger class sizes mandated by the new curricula became one of the points of tension with the traditional ABE discourse; it was not possible to individualise programs and to deliver student-centred education for 15–18 students.

For many the issue was a fundamental one of the inappropriateness of competency-based training for the field.

> I think part of the problem is that we've never been a complete fit with TAFE in some ways. I work [with LN learner support] in cookery and floristry and the assessments for them make sense ... because they have been taught these things, but reading isn't like that and there is no recognition that we are different, and what we teach is different ... (Robin – interview)

Assessment

The principles of competency-based assessment were integral to CBT. Assessment tools had to be devised to measure students' achievement of the competencies identified by industry, since one of the central pillars of the corporate management techniques that had been transferred to education was measurement of outputs. Although assessment of ABE students had been a source of tension in the field since the first introduction of an accredited course, without doubt one of the most contentious developments of the field from the end of the 1980s was this introduction of mandatory competency-based assessment and reporting frameworks.

> I can remember the energy ... that went into trying to develop these reporting frameworks, because we just kept getting messages from Canberra and from friends who were aware of what the changes were. .... The capability to understand assessment and how to report on assessment and how to understand and report on learning outcomes and so on – was all being driven by that message that if you can't do this, you're not going to get any funding. (Rosie – interview)

Whilst there was a recognition that this was the price to be paid for moving 'into the mainstream', vigorous debates ensued, centred around the possibility of assessing language, literacy and numeracy in a holistic way in this new context (Campbell 2009) and enormous amounts of intellectual energy were expended by practitioners and academics in the field in attempting to reconcile these seemingly irreconcilable requirements.

ABE programs had always developed their own assessment procedures and resources and follow-up processes similar to the earlier *How's it going?* approach (Good & Holmes 1979). These were student centred and holistic processes, designed to guide pedagogical decisions and to involve the learner. Robyn described her assessment process:

> What sort of evolved was, I had a portfolio for every student and all their work and all their drafts and all their writing were put together and we could look through it and discuss it and it was all related to what we were doing and that was useful and that made sense. (Interview)

The approach aimed to assess the *process* of reading, writing and calculating, as well as the *product* and to consider affective as well as cognitive change (Osmond 1989). However, this descriptive and student-centred approach to assessment was another of the profession's discourses that carried little weight with the new pipers; other forms of evidence of responsible use of public funds were required and these individualised reporting methods were not considered sufficient. As Lo Bianco told the audience at an ACAL conference in 1987, adult literacy practitioners, and the students themselves, understand the 'empowerment which literacy can bring to individual adults ... [However] in more powerful places it simply is not sufficient justification' (cited in Black 1995, p. 29).

In order for the profession to gain control of the educational products that would be required in this new context, academics and activists argued that the first step should be the articulation of an 'educationally defensible approach to describing adult English language, literacy, and numeracy competence in ways that could guide curriculum development and reporting' (Wickert et al. 2007, p. 258). The *National Accreditation Framework for English Language, Literacy and Numeracy Competence* (known as the *National Framework*) was developed by a team of language, literacy and numeracy (LLN) academics and professionals. The *Framework* was underpinned by notions of the social context of LLN. Rather than a skills-based or linear representation of skills, it aimed to represent the social and cultural complexity of LLN.

Although it was generally well received by the profession, there were critics who did not find it easily accessible. Nevertheless, Wickert et al. (2007) wrote that:

> despite this mixed impact, we consider it to be an important legacy of this period. It provided a strong counter resource for adult literacy and numeracy practitioners during a time of intense production of narrow, decontextualized lists of competencies as standards for industry training. (pp. 261–262)

However, although it was probably not well understood, the *National Framework* was generally well accepted in the field, mainly because it had been developed by ABE professionals and academics, and because there was a sense in which it legitimised the field theoretically. Anne recalled

> a sense of excitement that there was ... a theoretical underpinning being talked about that tried to reflect the complexity of what we did and somehow bring together the sociological, and the linguistic, and the student-centredness of what we did. It probably didn't work quite in that way and went over the top, but it was something that was trying to get to the essence and clarify the essence of what we were doing and why. (Interview)

An attempt to provide a reporting mechanism for individual LN proficiency and progress had been commissioned by the Commonwealth government in 1991 (Griffin & Forwood 1991), but was abandoned after only a very few trials amid professional dissatisfaction. The Commonwealth commissioned another attempt in 1994. This was the *National Reporting System* (NRS) (Coates et al. 1995) which was informed by the recently developed *National Framework* and aimed to capture the complexity of the competence statements contained in the *Framework*. The NRS thus attempted to provide 'the richest possible picture of competence ... based as closely as possible on a model reflecting real life performance' (p. 4). This was to become a template for further iterations of reporting mechanisms in future decades. Nevertheless, although most practitioners accepted their theoretical rigour, attempts to use these assessment frameworks as measurement and reporting mechanisms have always met with distrust and even hostility.

The NRS was essentially a framework for *describing* literacy and numeracy competence. It was inappropriate as a *measurement* tool, although that was the use that was required of it. Students enrolled in Commonwealth-funded courses would be required to do a pre- and post-course assessment, with much riding on the outcome for both the student and provider.

The very principle of assessment of literacy and numeracy student competencies continued to be resented and resisted, as were the compliance and reporting mechanisms that accompanied it. Many felt that these assessment processes were 'counter-active to why the people had come there, and that dilemma was never gotten over' (Brigid – interview). Importantly, the very concept of having to give an ABE student a 'fail' result was anathema to ABE's foundation principles. Teachers reported that they avoided recording a 'fail' result where possible and went to great lengths to manipulate enrolment processes and alternative result codes 'to avoid giving students this sense of failure and to give them the time they need' (Hazell 1998, p. 76). Robyn's recollection was that 'I think we just ignored it for a while. Everybody just passed. And I am still not sure that that is not a good idea' (Interview).

Brigid's complaint was typical of many interviewees:

> The accountability and assessment of students was huge and then that just went on and on and on till there was no more teaching done and it was all assessment. (Interview)

The complaints about the compliance requirements were perhaps the most bitter, with deep concern expressed over the time and professional energy spent on development of assessment tasks, validation, moderation and the threat of audit.

> It has been huge because of the impact it has had on us as a section. Everybody is frantic, constantly frantic about having [to] put together assessments and do assessments and – 'This form? And no, this one has to be this way, not that way. And what happens if they come and have a look?' (Robyn – interview)
>
> That's another of the changes that's so worrying – that head teachers are now entirely absorbed in the bureaucracy and administration and have no educational work to do and they are so bogged down in all this silly compliance stuff. It is madness. I just think the whole thing is Alice in Wonderland. Straight down the rabbit hole. It is mad. I really think it is frightening. (Margaret – interview)

78 *A new discourse emerges*

Many who had experienced the traditional, student-centred culture, simply resisted, a response that has been widely reported in the literature (for example, Black 2010; Sanguinetti 1999; Tusting 2009).

> Personally, I don't get as upset about it as other people do. I won't let it impinge on the way I teach. I won't do it. People say, 'what if we get audited – what if ...?' There is no doubt in my mind that I can justify what I do with these people educationally. I can do that. I know I can. You don't like it? That's it. Not doing it.
> (Robyn – interview)

The training market

Under the National Training Reform Agenda, the VET market had been opened up to private providers who wished to register as Registered Training Organisations (RTOs) to tender for public funding alongside the newly commercialised TAFE institutes. The imperative for teachers to comply with the new assessment and reporting requirements was the constant threat that their employer would lose the contract in the next round of tenders if the organisation was deemed to be non-compliant.

The competitive nature of the market-based approach was expected to advance the key objectives of the NTRA. These were to promote greater flexibility and diversity in responding to the needs of industry and national economic priorities, with an open training market that would increase the quality, efficiency and effectiveness of training (Anderson 1996). The main remaining difference between public and private training providers was that public providers were still allocated some recurrent funding, which, however, decreased with each successive budget.

The effect of this reform on public institutions such as TAFE was that large areas of the public sector became commercialised, either by applying the principles of market driven competition, or by contracting out their previous functions to market-based private providers. TAFE was required to operate on an equal playing ground with these new private providers. In an effort to make TAFE and other public institutions more competitive, constant restructuring was a feature of successive decades, as the archival evidence bears witness.

Adult basic education in Australia

In addition to the change wrought on ABE practice as an integral part of VET, it was to face further challenges specific to the sector. The late

1980s had represented a turning point in the development of the field. The economic utility of the field had been affirmed and it was clear that more secure forms of funding would follow. I have represented this period as a key *moment of translation* of many in the field to the new social project of re-ordering. Some in the field responded in very positive and optimistic terms about the new opportunities that were being offered with the move to the mainstream of VET. For example, at a forum organised by ACAL, one of the literacy pioneers and activists, then working for the recently formed Australian National Training Authority (ANTA), told the meeting,

> I see an enormous window of opportunity here for the field, because we are at the stage of developing new policy about funding. We can either get incredibly pessimistic and worry about how the money at the moment seems to be negating the needs of people with literacy problems; or we can say, okay, there is a space to slip into, and start to provide some solutions. (ACAL 1997, p. 56)

It was, however, a moment of *partial translation*, as this section shows. Many in the field felt and warned that it was a dangerous moment. In her prophetically titled article 'Resisting hijack and seduction' (1990), the Victorian adult literacy pioneer Helen Gribble warned that the 1990s would be a busy time for literacy activists, with the expectation of,

> [a] struggle against aggressive efforts to hijack our work, and more subtle efforts to persuade us that a vocationally specific approach is appropriate for adult literacy and basic education in the workplace. If we resist, there's hope for success. Surrendering to narrow vocationalism without a fight is unthinkable. (1990, p. 55)

What Gribble was warning against was an abandonment of the principles of adult basic education that had become central to the discourse of the field. This, she argued, would not lead to the development of the flexible, critically thinking workers that the new industrial environment would require.

Seddon (1994) has argued that the field had been able to develop its particular character and its many strengths simply because it had emerged outside of the educational mainstream. It had been able to develop 'a holistic, just and enlightening education because it has always been the "other" to mainstream education' (p. 9). Transferring this body of 'just and enlightening' professional practice knowledge to the mainstream of VET was not going to be easy and the option of being left alone to develop programs that were responsive to the needs of the students was, in many senses, an attractive, if unlikely proposition (Wickert & Zimmerman 1991). Rosie referred to 'that plus/minus element of gaining recognition' (Interview).

The main concerns continued to be not only with this new role that ABE would play in VET, but with the abandonment of the field's traditional student base and the educational philosophy that supported it. The theme of the 1989 NSWALC conference was *Vocational Literacy – New Directions, New Decisions*. Following several days' talk of workplace and vocational education, one of the conference resolutions was that 'the rights of community students to have access to adult literacy and numeracy programs is not endangered by the emphasis on skills training and vocational literacy' (NSW Adult Literacy Council 1989, p. 7).

The concern was for continuation of provision for non-jobseekers (also referred to as community students), such as those who were carers, those wishing to improve their parenting skills or to support their children's school work, or those who could not or did not wish to join the workforce. This sentiment was echoed in Wickert and Zimmerman's (1991, p. 193) assertion that 'the need to ally ourselves to the new agenda is imperative. To do that with integrity is our challenge'. Many urged the need to learn the new language of human capital while retaining the field's 'own cultural identity and values' (Zimmerman & Norton 1990, p. 144). This remained a tension in the field for the remainder of the decade and beyond and is an expression of the central theme of this book: the transition from the earlier humanist, social justice discourse to the present human capital discourse surrounding the field.

A new national policy

As the three year funding recommended by the *National Policy on Languages* was coming to its end, adult literacy activists began to agitate for a new policy and renewal of the funding. Eventually, after much lobbying from the field, the Commonwealth Government committed itself to a successor to the *National Policy on Languages*. This was the *Australian Language and Literacy Policy* (ALLP) (DEET 1991), a significant policy and funding commitment and an important *moment* in the narrative for several reasons: the commitment of considerable funds and the clear signal of changed priorities. In the opening paragraph of the ALLP, the alliance with the now dominant human capital discourse is spelt out:

Global economic forces are demanding changes in the structure of Australian industry, in our ability to compete in world markets and in our readiness to adapt to new jobs, new career structures and new technologies. These changes will require new skills in communication, understanding and cultural awareness, in the workplace as much as in the international marketplace. They will also place added pressures on our education and training systems. (DEET, cited in Black 1995, p. 34)

The funding made available under the ALLP confirmed the government's economic priority. The areas of jobseeker and workplace literacy that had received some earlier funding now received very significant increases; they were the centrepiece of the policy and came to obscure other equity driven non-employment-related programs.

Jobseekers

The jobseeker program funded under the ALLP was part of the government's new Active Employment Strategy which ensured that jobseekers with fundamental literacy difficulties would be sent to literacy/numeracy classes for assistance. This was called the *Special Intervention Program* (SIP).

The advent of these Commonwealth-funded jobseeker programs had coincided with and was undoubtedly influenced by the OECD's Active Society policy. This promoted an expectation that welfare recipients engage in welfare-to-work programs or otherwise show that they were developing work capabilities in exchange for welfare payments (Wickert et al. 2007). In Australia this policy became known as mutual obligation. The jobseekers, for their part were required to sign an agreement with the Commonwealth Employment Service (CES) agreeing to undertake an education or training program in order to improve their employment prospects. Thus, the SIP program was to deliver to literacy providers, many students with radically different motivation from those who were self-referred. Many were reluctant attendees with unhelpful views of themselves as learners, thus posing new challenges for ABE staff (Black 1995; Zimmerman & Norton 1990). 'For the first time we had people sent to us who didn't necessarily want to be there. That was a big major change in the flavour' (Sam – interview).

The relationship between ABE staff and their students changed radically in another important aspect also. A third party was introduced into the relationship; students and ABE staff alike became answerable to government agencies. Under new arrangements jobseekers would be referred by and monitored by CES officers. Teachers were now required to report on their attendance. If they failed to attend, they would be 'breached' and their benefits discontinued (DEET, cited in Black 1995, p. 23).

The election of the Howard conservative government in 1996 saw a shift in and further tightening of the regulations surrounding the Commonwealth-funded jobseeker program, with the creation of a new jobseeker program, the *Literacy and Numeracy Training* (LANT) program. The LANT program was placed within the labour market programs with their strong mutual obligation focus and although the earlier SIP program had also been underpinned by the notion of mutual obligation, it was not expressed as overtly as it was with the LANT program. It was felt that the earlier program had expressed mutual obligation within the policy context of a 'social justice approach' (Falk 2001, p. 212).

The language used to announce the new program gives an indication of the ways in which the government conceived of its relationship with the students or 'clients'. For example, Minister Kemp's press release suggests strongly the discourse of individual responsibility, deficit and blame that was to characterise the program:

> All people aged between 18 and 24 who have been receiving unemployment benefits for six months or more must now do more to help themselves find work or risk having their payments reduced or possibly withdrawn. Those who are assessed as having inadequate literacy or numeracy skills must undertake the training. Refusal could lead to an initial reduction of unemployment benefits of 18 per cent for 26 weeks. (cited in Manwaring & O'Maley 2001, p. 14)

Prime Minister Howard's announcement of the LANT program in his 1999 Address to the Nation, titled *The Australian Way*, further highlighted the government's punitive views of literacy in relation to unemployment:

> This government will require young people who lack basic literacy and numeracy skills to undertake training in those areas as a condition of receiving their full unemployment benefit. Refusing to learn how to read and write will deny young unemployed the full dole. (cited in Manwaring & O'Maley 2001, p. 14)

A new discourse emerges 83

The LANT program went through other iterations and in 2013 it was replaced by the *Skills for Education and Employment* (SEE) program. These various versions of the jobseeker program had been overseen by successive conservative and Labor governments, with little change in their philosophical orientation or operation. However, towards the end of this period the competitive tendering process to determine allocation of program contracts became more and more responsive to the conservative government's free market approach, with contracts increasingly awarded to private providers, including novice providers in the field, and international corporations.

Along with changes to the jobseeker education programs came radical changes to the jobseeker referral agencies that were responsible for initial assessment and referral of clients. The functions of the CES, the government department that had originally performed this function, were also tendered out to private and semi-government organisations.

With the profit motive driving referral and provision, many prospective students were being denied the opportunity to participate even in this provision. A 2015 SEE program evaluation found that many agencies 'lack an understanding of the SEE programme, the referral process and/or how to identify LLN needs in clients' (Acil Allen Consulting 2015, p. 35). Referrals to employment attracted higher levels of remuneration to the agency than referrals to and completion of literacy/ numeracy (LN) training programs. The evaluation showed that many clients were encouraged by their referring agencies to exit their SEE program early in order to accept employment, rather than continue to develop their LLN skills, 'to the detriment of their long-term employability' (Acil Allen Consulting 2015, p. 59). Marketisation had become an unwelcome intrusion into adults' opportunities for a basic education.

Prospective students were also denied access to the program on the grounds that they were unlikely to make sufficient progress. This was justified on the grounds that the eligibility criteria for the program stated that eligible clients are those that 'are deemed suitable for training without any barriers that would prevent successful participation' (DESE 2020). Successful participation was interpreted as being job-ready within the short period allocated to the training program. Thus, many adults who were assessed as having lower skill levels were to be denied access to the main source of publicly funded provision, on the grounds that engaging in literacy tuition would not lead to increased human capital. In reference to a similar employment-related program in Canada, Darville (2011) referred to 'these invidious cost-benefit calculations [that make] lower level people appear as costly investments with unlikely pay-off' (p. 167).

Workplace

The proposition that the field of adult literacy should be the concern of more than just the education community had always been evident in the professional discourse. It was seen as a community-wide issue that should involve a range of community members and agencies, including employers. In fact this community development approach, involving many sectors of the community, was the vision of Arch Nelson and other pioneers of the field (Nelson 1985) as discussed in Chapter 3.

In 1989 ACAL began coordinating a national awareness campaign to highlight the need for wider, non-government involvement in adult literacy programs in the lead-up to International Literacy Year (ILY) (ACAL 1989). It is not surprising that engagement with workplace literacy and numeracy issues should become part of the professional discourse since issues related to the workplace served to highlight the contextual nature of literacy and numeracy skills. The field was therefore philosophically open to the idea when engagement with workplace literacy/numeracy development became an imperative; the field was quickly and easily mobilised into the new network.

Further encouragement was of a pragmatic nature. The public provider's recurrent funding had been progressively diminishing and it had now been positioned as a market player, competing in industry's newly articulated education and training market. As with the contract for jobseeker programs, there was also financial advantage and institutional kudos for ABE staff that came from involvement with workplace programs. This engagement of ABE practitioners with industry training was further accelerated with the introduction of the Commonwealth-funded Workplace English Language and Literacy (WELL) program in 1991.

Anne remembered 'when this [workplace LN] suddenly came wheeling with a great head of steam' (Interview) and a number of the interviewees recalled the sense that it had become the 'flavour of the month' and that workplace activity had become the new, 'sexy' face of ABE.

> When it first started to be talked about there was an attitude of, if you weren't doing it, who were you? I think it was a bit of a shock to the system in the beginning, but some people leapt on it.
> (Alison – interview)

From the beginning there had been concern amongst practitioners about the nature and purpose of workplace LN. Is the program just to do the bidding of management in order to improve their economic position, or could the needs of the workers continue to be considered as had been the tradition of ABE practice? There were a range of responses to this tension in the discourse.

> We expected a company to allow a group of their workers to stop working and sit round in a group and do traditional ABE stuff. It was a joke. You go out there as a teacher – who is your boss? ... In the end the agenda shifted more and more to precisely, exactly what the boss wanted. (Sam – interview)

It soon became clear that workplace education would be seen as another version of the LN learner support program for students enrolled in VET courses, a program that had been a central aspect of the ABE provision in TAFE colleges. There was an argument that workplace education worked best when it supported a workplace qualification.

> It's a bit of a waste of time trying to do on-the-job things that aren't actually related to a workplace qualification. (Anne – interview)

Anne's comment suggests that most teachers who continued to practice in workplace education contexts had accepted the changed nature and needs of this new student group for whom most of the principles of the Adult Literacy Discourse were considered not to be relevant, and had adjusted their teaching principles accordingly. Most interviewees agreed, however, that there were a number of incidental outcomes for the workers that were consistent with traditional ABE principles, although it depended on the relationship that existed between the teacher and the workers.

> what often happens in workplace situations is that the people in there ... get this feeling over time that these trainers are coming in to help them with their jobs so 'I must be worth something'. I think that doesn't always happen, but it happens a fair bit. (Alison – interview)
> Some of those guys told me that they actually went home and read to their children for the first time because of their engagement in ... reading for the work process. (Joanne – interview)

Even in spite of the money and the kudos that it brought in the college, many ABE teachers reported that they had avoided involvement in workplace programs. Jan's attitude was probably typical of many colleagues:

> I preferred to work for students' individual social needs rather than an employer's needs. And we used to kid ourselves that we were meeting their individual needs [in a workplace program] ... essentially it was so the employer could make more money. So I was never a big workplace person. (Interview)

Provision for the traditional learner group that Jan referred to, however, was being progressively withdrawn and it was apparent to interviewees such as Jan that none of the principles of the Adult Literacy Discourse had found a place in the new discourse of workplace and vocational education.

A forced marriage

The language used to delineate the field changed in this era also. The term adult basic education ceased to be used (except in the professional discourse) and language, literacy and numeracy (LLN) became more entrenched in the lexicon. Under that acronym the fields of adult basic education and adult ESOL (English for Speakers of Other Languages) were forced into close collaboration in the development of the *National Framework* discussed above.

The effort to articulate a theoretical base in the development of these frameworks and reporting systems was to bring the fields of adult literacy and adult ESOL into a closer working relationship, since the two fields had been brought together administratively under the *Australian Language and Literacy Policy*. Whilst there had always been a warm collegiate relationship between the two fields, especially during the foundation years of adult literacy in NSW (see Chapter 3), they were now required to reconcile their respective theoretical understandings. A report on the *Pedagogical Relations Between Adult ESL and Adult Literacy* (Hammond et al. 1992) analysed the similarities and differences between the two fields with the conclusion that they both drew on similar theories of language and literacy teaching, with the major difference being in the 'nature and needs of ESL and adult literacy learners' (Hammond & Wickert 1993, p. 22). A difference in educational philosophy is implicated by this difference in target learner groups; the strong humanist, student-centred approach of ABE was not necessarily a part of the tradition from which ESOL had emerged. Baynham (1991) had written that

The reason why educational fields develop as they do is due to a complex interrelation of historical, political and economic factors ... Simply establishing a theoretical basis for the 'common ground' is to a certain extent a naïve exercise. (p. 5)

As Hammond and Wickert acknowledged, 'tensions emerge as the pressure for closer working arrangements intensifies as a result of economic and political imperatives within increasingly centralist government practices' (1993, p. 17). The earlier collegial collaborative relationship between the two fields became one of tension and competition in this era, as government attempted a forced and uneasy 'marriage' between the two. This is perhaps the point at which the field of adult ESOL became a *dissident* (Callon 1986, p. 219) in the previous actor network that had assisted in the genesis of the new field of ABE. Although, as a fellow sector of the adult education field, its interests were remarkably similar to those of ABE, the tensions were such that they no longer saw themselves as part of the same actor network.

Integration

The term integration entered the professional discourse in the early 1990s. Industry bodies and the advisory bodies that had been created to guide and support the development of vocational competencies all agreed that literacy, numeracy and other communication skills were an important element in success training and career advancement.

The integration of literacy/numeracy into VET therefore became central to the adult literacy policy discourse and was to have important implications for the very definition of literacy/numeracy as the decades progressed.

In 1994, in recognition of the position that the concept of integration had gained in the discourse around VET, TAFE NSW commissioned a report which defined integration thus:

> Integrating English language, literacy and numeracy and vocational competence as interrelated elements of the one process. This involves designing and delivering programs which meet the skills needs of the job or occupation, and which are responsive to the diversity of learners' skills, needs and resources. (Courtenay & Mawer 1995, p. 2)

One of Courtenay and Mawer's key recommendations was that literacy and numeracy development should be the responsibility of vocational education and training as a whole, and not remain the responsibility of LLN specialists alone. For this reason, they recommended that 'programs should be supported by strategies to develop the knowledge and skills of education and training practitioners in responding appropriately to language, literacy and numeracy factors in vocational education and training' (1995, p. 8).

Thus, they were encouraging a new group of actors to be *mobilised* and *enrolled* into the actor network that was engaged in re-imagining adult basic education within VET. The success of the project however, was short term, but with lasting unintended consequences.

This integration of LLN with VET was hastened with the election in 1996 of the Howard conservative government, bringing to an end 'Australia's literacy decade' (McKenna & Fitzpatrick 2004, p. 68). The new government signalled that it intended to further streamline the reform of the vocational training process that had begun in the late 1980s with processes and guidelines that became increasingly more stringent and allied to the neoliberal agenda.

For the field of ABE, the key element of interest in the new reforms was the introduction of *training packages*. These aimed at establishing a framework of industry standards for each industry grouping, packaged to form a range of national qualifications. The standards were developed by Industry Training Advisory Bodies (ITABS), further enhancing the role of industry in determining the skills taught and assessed in the education sector and moving the centre of influence over vocational education ever more closely to industry. In the face of this shift, an enormous amount of professional energy in the adult literacy field was expended by those who enthusiastically engaged in the *translation* to the new ABE project within VET, aiming to ensure that issues of LLN were taken into account in the development of training packages in vocational fields.

The development of training packages was shown to have far-reaching implications for many practitioners of adult language, literacy and numeracy who were to become deeply involved in the VET reforms of this period. Wignall, who was close to these changes, wrote that:

> The changes will mean new ways of working within industry assessing and reporting against Industry Standards using the new Training Packages. For others, the changes may be far broader and may mean a complete reassessment of their role as a language, literacy and numeracy practitioner or the need for additional training. Either way, there will be many new things to know, and an adjustment of all the useful skills, training and assessment you've acquired under the 'old' system to fit in with the new system. (1999, p. 7)

In order to address these 'new ways of working within industry', the ANTA *Workplace Communication Project* was established and produced professional development packages and resources to ensure that LLN was integrated into training package delivery. Significant amongst these products was the publication of *Built in, not bolted on* (Wignall 1999) which became a key resource to demonstrate the ways in which language, literacy and numeracy could be integrated into vocational competencies.

To further ensure integration of LLN with the new competency-based training, a new Certificate IV in Training and Assessment (TAE) package for vocational teachers and trainers was developed, specifically integrating LLN across all the units and adding a specialist LLN unit. The intention was that all VET trainers and assessors would develop the competency to identify learners who may need LLN support and to be able to develop strategies to support such learners.

This move to integrate LLN into vocational training, which had begun to accelerate in the 1990s, became central to the professional discourse in this period. As Wignall had suggested in her discussion of the role of LLN teachers in industry, 'If you're not in the vanguard you are in the guard's van' (Wignall 1999, p. 22).

Although integration had become central to the professional discourse, the literature shows that many in the field were sceptical of its ultimate success, given the primary focus on skills development in the VET sector (for example, Sanguinetti 2007; Wickert et al. 2007). The findings of a number of research projects into the effects of integrating literacy and numeracy into training packages (for example, Sanguinetti & Hartley 2000) suggested that, in spite of the efforts of literacy practitioners and activists, VET trainers continued to pay little attention to the LLN needs of the trainees, and there was a wide-spread under-usage of the range of ANTA developed materials that could have supported the integration of literacy/numeracy into training. The literacy practitioners and activists were ultimately not powerful entities within this new network.

Outsourced foundation skills products

In 2004 adult basic education (now called Foundation Skills) was included under one of the industry boards that determined the industry competencies and managed the development of VET curriculum. Thereafter the field gained a training package, *Training and Education* (TAE), containing three teaching qualifications:

- Certificate IV in Training and Assessment
- Vocational Graduate Certificate in Adult Language, Literacy and Numeracy Practice (later to become the Graduate Diploma of Adult Language, Literacy and Numeracy Practice)
- Graduate Diploma of Adult Language, Literacy and Numeracy Leadership.

These qualifications were focussed entirely on training teachers to work in the vocational context with a heavy emphasis on assessment. The previous tertiary level qualifications that had fed the professional practice knowledge of earlier decades began to be withdrawn so that apart from one other university qualification, the only specialist adult literacy/numeracy teaching qualification was that contained in the TAE training package, and developed by an industry body. The fact that it was developed by the VET sector and focussed on meeting the immediate needs of practitioners (as required of a training package) severely curtailed the scope of the qualification and excluded, for example, 'places and spaces for teachers to engage in critical inquiry to change and develop their practices' (Yasukawa 2010, p. 85). In 2016 responsibility for foundation skills was moved to PricewaterhouseCoopers (PwC), a multinational accounting and professional services corporation. Thus, the government had outsourced policy and curriculum development for ABE and further distanced it from the influence of practitioners. Having laid down tight parameters, the governance of the field was thus ceded to the market.

In 2013 another training package was developed for VET students, the *Foundation Skills Training Package* (FSK) (IBSA 2013) It was designed to support students enrolled in VET courses who struggle with the LN requirements of those courses. This was soon to become the major LN curriculum in use in the state. Crucially, it did not specify specialist adult basic education qualifications as a requirement to deliver the FSK. Rather, it stated that trainers and assessors 'will require recognised expertise in the delivery and assessment of foundation skills. This expertise will vary according to the training context and the needs of the learners' (IBSA 2013, p. 6). This downgrading (and removal) of the specialist qualifications required to teach foundation skills was the result of direct influence of industry, in this case the education and training industry that had in recent years been expanded to include a large number of private providers. They had joined the network of actors shaping the field, and had developed a powerful voice, as demonstrated by the following statement by one of the developers of the FSK training package in reference to the outcome of the consultations with stakeholders:

Some LLN practitioners would like to see delivery from the FSK restricted to qualified LLN teachers, but many stakeholders feel that less stringent requirements are necessary if the package is to be taken up in the broad range of delivery environments for which it is intended. (Roberts 2013, p. 15)

The evidence shows the dismay of the profession that, at the request of the private training market, a large sector of provision in the field now did not require specialist qualifications for its teachers (for example, NSW Adult Literacy & Numeracy Council 2018).

A new national strategy

Twenty years since the previous major policy initiative, a new product was launched in 2012; this was the *National Foundation Skills Strategy Project* (SCOTESE 2012). Recognition was given in the document of the need to assist individuals to develop their foundation skills for both social and economic purposes, in the interests of the individual, of civil society and of the national economy. This was articulated in the vision for the strategy, which was to support:

> A proactive and inclusive Australia in which adults develop and maintain the foundation skills they need to participate confidently in the economy and meet the complex demands of modern life. (p. 9)

Recognition was given at various points in the document also to the role of literacy development in social capacity building, for example:

> Australian governments also recognise the benefits that improved foundation skills can deliver to individuals and the community through enriched personal lives and greater community participation. (p. 4)

Moreover, the elaboration of one of the key priority areas for action is consistent with the traditional, student-centred principles of adult literacy practice. It recommended that:

> Adult learners have high quality learning opportunities and outcomes – providing a variety of foundation skills development opportunities that can be tailored to individual needs will make it easier for learners to build skills that are relevant to their situation. (p. 3)

92 A new discourse emerges

However, a critical reading of the document clarifies the predominant discourse surrounding it. The opening sentence of the ministerial foreword signals the intent: 'More than 7.5 million Australian adults do not have the literacy and numeracy skills needed to participate fully in today's workforce' (p. i). The foreword makes no mention of any objectives for the strategy, other than human capital objectives. The site chosen for the launch of the strategy provides further evidence: it was launched by the Parliamentary Secretary for Education and Skills at an electronics factory (Yasukawa & Black 2016). The title of the strategy had a powerful message to send also: the field was to be known as *Foundation Skills* with little acknowledgement of the social context view of literacy.

The strategy comprised a small number of projects, most of which focussed on integration of LLN in VET (SCOTESE 2012). Crucially, there was no on-going or significant funding attached to this strategy, unlike the previous policies of the late 1980s and early 1990s. It was therefore an aspirational document, open to market forces to determine the areas in which and the extent to which it was implemented. Given the evidence of government's faith in market forces to indicate funding allocations, the influence of industry bodies continued to ensure that funding was allocated almost exclusively to employment-related programs to the exclusion of other priorities suggested in the document.

The new literacy/numeracy actor network

It is not surprising that the human capital message emerged as the prominent message from the NFSS since the coalition of industry interests that were driving the direction of the field had shown an interest in the Strategy from its inception. For example, the Australian Industry Group commissioned a study, *When words fail* (2012), to investigate the views of employers regarding the literacy levels of their employees, and showed, predictably, that '75% of employers reported that their business was affected by low levels of literacy and numeracy' (p. ii), with the recommendation that employers' views and concerns be positioned 'at the centre of the *National Foundation Skills Strategy*' (p. vi). Thus the new Strategy added its authority to the literacy/numeracy-as-human-capital message that continued to be voiced by a number of entities in the new actor network (for example, Australian Industry Group 2015, 2016; Shomos 2010; Skills Australia 2011). These key players were all heeding the advice of the then head of the skills policy advisory body to ensure they were 'singing from the same hymn sheet' (cited in Yasukawa & Black 2016, p. 33),

Deprofessionalising the profession

A project to develop a *Foundation Skills Professional Standards Framework* (Wignall Consulting Services 2017) was one of the recommendations of the National Foundation Skills Strategy and was the response to the fourth of its key priority areas: 'Building the capacity of the education and training workforces to deliver foundation skills' (SCOTESE 2012, p. 3). The Framework encompassed a wide range of contexts and functions of those involved in the delivery of foundation skills, from 'people for whom foundation skills provision is their whole job' to 'people for whom responsibility for addressing foundation skills is a subset of their broader teaching, training and assessing practice' (Wignall Consulting Services 2017, pp. 2–3). The fact that it attempts to describe this diversity of the field makes it a key source document for an understanding of the way the field is framed in the new millennium.

There is no clear demarcation in the document between specialist foundation skills teachers and those who play a support role, thus further strengthening the perception within VET that ABE is not a specialist field and does not require specialist qualifications, and hereby diminishing the status of the profession. The diversity of contexts and roles that the document encompasses suggests that it is now difficult to refer to the *field* of adult basic education, or even the *field* of foundation skills. Attention to foundation skills occurs in such a range of VET and non-VET contexts and is the responsibility of such a range of people that, as a field, it has been rendered invisible.

At the time of writing, workforce planning for the foundation skills workforce seems to be in crisis. Much expertise had been lost with the retirement of many specialist trained teachers of the previous era. A series of TAFE restructures had seen the previous ABE sections amalgamated with others under the banner of Foundation Skills, and under generic managers many of whom have little or no understanding of the challenges faced by the field and its target students. Expertise began to be lost and the identity of the previous ABE field became invisible. Lorraine told of one TAFE metropolitan institute that had offered so many redundancy packages to its ABE staff in its efforts to restructure that it now found it was unable to offer the courses it wanted to because it didn't have the appropriate staff.

> There has been such an exodus, either because of 'efficiencies' or because people have just left, that even though there's now some funding where we can have an opportunity to do work, we're not

able to do that, so that's a real issue for us, finding and rebuilding that expertise. (Interview)

The community of practice begins to fracture

The 1990s saw the beginning of a fundamental change in the nature of the community of practice that had been a characteristic of the field in the previous era. For some years there was still evidence of its influence, both within the profession and politically. However, by the end of the decade it had become fractured with significant loss of influence.

The early part of the decade had seen unparalleled increase in funding for professional development, development of resources and research, all of which served as a glue for the community of practice. Anne spoke of this connection with the field as being:

> officially supported and developed by regular meetings, funded conferences, newsletters, coordinators – all of the keeping-in-touch, meeting face-to-face, all of those things – the value of it was explicitly recognised [by management and by government]. (Interview)

However, towards the latter part of the 1990s, this funding began to be withdrawn. The recurrent funding that the states had received to fund VET through public providers such as TAFE and Adult and Community Education (ACE) was cut severely, with the result that the traditional non-jobseeker ABE classes that did not receive Commonwealth jobseeker funding were the target of severe cut-backs. This was felt most severely in rural areas and small towns where one or two ABE classes a week may have been cut to none.

This shrinking of the traditional provision in the field was accompanied by sudden growth in the Commonwealth-funded jobseeker programs and the introduction of private providers to the field. The result was a rapid increase in the casualisation of the field which, as most interviewees agreed, added to the weakening of the community of practice.

Teachers with insecure employment were working across a number of providers or sites, with little time or appetite for the sharing culture of the past. The earlier workforce employed by the public provider had been public servants, many with secure, permanent employment; at the time of writing, most are employed by private providers in non-unionised, casualised employment. The constant restructuring of TAFE fractured even the TAFE ABE community of practice. Alison agreed that the fact that 'we are much more in our silos than ever … has a lot to do with the way the colleges and the institute is structured' (Interview).

A new discourse emerges 95

The onerous audit culture also continued to deflect attention from conversations around learner needs and professional responses to those needs. Rose argued that the compliance and accountability requirements 'takes far more time to do that than you've got to teach ... The accountability of it is down to fine print often for no legitimate outcome' (Interview).

The following response to my question about a sense of belonging to a community of practice is typical of the responses of all my interviewees:

> When I began there was such a strong community of practice at all levels ... all of that was officially supported ... And then the centralised TAFE system was broken into bits and we saw less of each other and there were less meetings and there was no longer a [state ABE] coordinator, and just simple things like there was no longer a state [ABE] staff list, just simple clerical things like that. So now nobody knows who is working in the field, and nobody ever gets to talk to each other. (Anne – interview)

The NSWALNC began to struggle for membership; in particular, for committed, active members, a situation that appears common to other state literacy councils from that time (Campbell 2005). In 2009 it almost faced closure. Anne, who had been president at one time reflected that:

> In the end it became almost impossible to run the council. It came down to the goodwill of three people ... but when it came to the crunch, unless people saw a value or were interested in taking part, what was the point? (Interview)

Interviewees gave a number of reasons for this lack of active interest, including the casualisation of the workforce, job losses and a sense of just needing to survive in an ever-changing environment. 'It just became a matter of surviving and dealing with the latest thing – wave of admin or policy that came through' (Anne – interview). There were also suggestions that practitioners no longer have a sense of what holds them together, and what is worth fighting for, or even possible to fight for. 'I don't actually know what I am pushing for, what I am fighting for ... and I am powerless to do anything about it [anyway]' (Sam – interview).

Amongst the cohesive factors that fed the original community of practice, specialist adult LN journals were mentioned as one of the important factors influencing the development of professional practice knowledge. In this era however, they began to disappear. ALIO's funding ceased in 2000, and, with its demise, its journal *Broadsheet* also came to an end. The NSWALNC journal *Literacy and Numeracy Exchange* was discontinued and became an e-newsletter, as did ACAL's journal *Literacy Links* The international journal *Literacy and Numeracy Studies* moved to an online publication and only VALBEC's *Fine Print* remained as a hard copy journal.

The scholarly underpinning that fed the body of professional practice knowledge also began to disappear. Funding to NCVER for adult literacy research was withdrawn in 2007 and as tertiary institutions began to discontinue their post-graduate adult LN courses, those academics who had been responsible for much national research and policy activism vacated the field. In 2015 the University of Technology Sydney (UTS), which had trained many specialist LN teachers in NSW, also discontinued its highly valued post-graduate course. For Rosie, this was one of the low points for the field:

> And of course, the demise of adult literacy teaching opportunities at higher education level, the demise of all the courses, that's a low. I think that was the lowest of the low, when the cert 4 [in Training and Assessment] became the requirement for teaching in ABE. (Interview)

The readily available professional development programs of past decades also fed the body of professional practice knowledge and helped to tie the community of practice together. With the demise of ALIO much of this also disappeared. Professional development was now the responsibility of individual providers and individual TAFE institutes.

Institute-based and college-based staff meetings or seminars came to be concentrated almost exclusively on assessment and compliance issues. When asked about these meetings, Anne replied, 'Never about content. And when I say never, I mean never. They're just always about computer systems'. Sonia agreed:

> Well so much of it seems to be driven by audit requirements and the reasons for doing assessment moderations and validations; having meetings to discuss our validation plans and our assessment plans; the number of assignments that we set; and the assessment tasks that we set – mostly around the threat of an audit rather than anything meaningful. (Interview)

The prominence of compliance and systems issues in the guise of professional development was indicated also in a survey of the LLN and education and training workforces which found that

The content areas of professional development most often undertaken by respondents in their current role related to: reporting and systems compliance; using new resources; learning about new delivery modes/methods; digital literacy and integrating LLN into vocational contexts. (Circelli 2015, p. 38)

The main locus of influence on the professional practice knowledge of the field had therefore shifted from the practitioners themselves in their sharing of professional craft knowledge (or bottom-up influence), to the government and institution level in their quest for assessment and systems evaluation information (top-down influences). Interviewee responses showed that they resented the fact that this had begun to appear as the important element of 'what counts' in professional practice knowledge.

The NSWALNC had continued to organise annual low-budget conferences but employer-funding for practitioners to attend had become very limited.

> Budgets started getting cut in institutes so that they wouldn't fund teachers to come to things even if they were coming in their own time. (Anne – interview)

Interviewees expressed a reluctance to continue to fund their own professional development, with a suggestion of growing loss of goodwill towards the employer:

> I have paid for professional development myself and conferences and webinars and things, but I am getting a bit jaded and I'm not shelling out that money any more. I want to learn but ... (Susan – interview)

Susan went on to argue, as many other interviewees did, that the casualisation of the workforce was one of the major factors providing a barrier to the creativity that had fed the community of practice in previous decades:

> I think it's a very dangerous way to run an education business. Because, I'm casual, I'm paid for the hours I teach so nearly everything else I put in is free. So I can do that for a while, but I can't do that forever ... And you feel like they [the employers] don't care. (Interview)

The sense of agency that the profession had over its development also diminished in this era, from a high point when professionals were actively consulted on the development of the *National Policy on Languages* and the projects that were funded under it. By the end of the 1990s these consultations were tokenistic, and the views of the profession were no longer actively sought in the development of policy.

The fate of the much-loved periodical *Good practice in Australian adult literacy and basic education* (Shipway 1988–1991) demonstrated the decline of the hands-on, personal involvement of the community of practice. *Good practice* had appeared in 1988 with Commonwealth funding and until 1992 it was edited by practitioners in the field, with articles contributed by practitioners. In 1993, in line with the new marketisation of government, the government department that funded it insisted that it be tendered out to a commercial publishing house for management, including editorship. Haughton, one of Victoria's pioneers in the field who had herself been an editor, wrote that:

> Outcry from the field erupted. The topics for each issue for the next four years mostly reflected DEET's funding priorities; advertorials increased ... The overall number of articles offered by practitioners declined markedly. (Haughton 2000, p. 7)

This was a period of professionalisation of the field but ironically, it was a shift that was not entirely welcomed by the community of practice. The DIY nature of the sharing of professional practice knowledge of the earlier years had helped to create the sense of belonging and ownership of the profession and this slowly ceased to be an influence. In addition, there was resentment towards the very nature of the new context of provision and a curriculum framework that was based on a conservative, skills-based view of language. Practitioners had begun to feel alienated from the field itself.

Adult Literacy Information Office (ALIO)

The previous chapter indicated that the story of ALIO was in many important ways symbolic of the story of ABE in NSW in particular. It paralleled also the developments of VET in Australia, so its trajectory is an important and interesting one to trace. In the study of the *Rise and fall of the NSW Adult Literacy and Information Office* (Johnston, Kelly & Johnston 2001, p. 8), the authors characterised its early years in the 1980s as operating 'on the smell of an oily

A new discourse emerges 99

rag', but by the next decade, it was the recipient of 'dollars and hoops to jump through' leading to 'professionalism' and ultimately its closure in late 1999.

Along with TAFE, ALIO had been restructured to respond to the demands of the National Training Reform agenda. Its new mission statement, published in 1993 was to 'enhance the quality of adult basic education provision in line with national and state education and training priorities' (Broadsheet 37 cited in Johnston, Kelly & Johnston 2001, p. 10). This signalled a paradigm shift in its strategic direction, along with the rest of TAFE NSW.

This demise of ALIO was emblematic of the field in general. It had been a joint Commonwealth and NSW government funded initiative but the Commonwealth funding for research and professional development projects which it had relied on began to dry up and the NSW government was unable and unwilling to add to ALIO's funding. (Its contribution had been to fund the salaries and running costs.) The fact that ALIO's charter was to support all providers now posed a problem for TAFE (who had managed it on behalf of the NSW government) in this era of competitive contestable funding. TAFE, through ALIO, was now sponsoring professional development and other services to its competitors, a situation that TAFE management could no longer support (Johnston, Kelly & Johnston 2001).

Even the fact that it was allowed to close silently, and with very little reaction from the field, was symbolic of the time. This was in contrast to earlier announcements of unwelcome changes (for example, the threat of the imposition of fees on ABE students) that brought the community of practice into action, invariably with a positive outcome. By now that once active community of practice was mute. Private providers had entered the field with a casualised workforce and TAFE had faced constant restructuring so that even TAFE ABE networks were weakened.

Johnston et al. (2001) argue that a further reason for the silence accompanying its closure was, paradoxically, the eventual professionalisation of ALIO. Although the wealth of professional development opportunities that it had offered had been warmly welcomed and appreciated, in many ways teachers no longer shared the sense of ownership of ALIO that had characterised its earlier years.

Nevertheless, many would undoubtedly have agreed with Fiona that the low point in the narrative of the field was marked 'when ALIO closed' (Interview).

Discussion and conclusion

By the beginning of the new millennium, the field had certainly consolidated its position by being drawn into the argument for the importance of vocational education in protecting the nation's economic prosperity. A monetary value had been placed on literacy so that its place in the policy and public discourse of the nation was assured. However, this brought with it a tension between the discourse of social justice (which was still evident in the professional discourse and rhetoric of policy documents during this era) and the public discourse of human capital and employment driven provision. Ultimately the human capital argument began to overshadow any other argument for the provision of adult basic education services.

This was driven by the increasingly powerful network of actors that had begun to gather around ABE in the 1990s and became even more adept in delivering a coordinated message in the new millennium. Prominent among them were the industry bodies that had been drawn in by government to drive the VET reforms of this era. With the increasing marketisation of the training field, this dominant actor network was also joined by the private training provider lobby. The actor network that had shaped the direction of the field in previous decades (which included academics and practitioners from the field) was voiceless in this re-problematised social project of literacy as human capital.

Although the human capital argument had always been an intrinsic element in the discourses around adult basic education, the dominance of neoliberal ideas driving government ensured its increasing predominance. Practitioners resented the effects of the marketisation of the field, the casualisation of the workforce and the stultifying effect of ever-increasing compliance requirements that served to remove any trace of the previous humanist Adult Literacy Discourse from provision. The new discourses had little to say about classroom practice. Discussion about assessment protocols had moved into the space vacated by genuine discussions of teaching and learning practice.

The contested arena of student assessment became one of irreconcilable tension between the professional and the policy discourse. In the earlier era of internal professional accountability, practitioners had a sense that they owed that accountability principally to their students. The indicators of performance that the field generally agreed upon in that era (and to a lesser extent, today) related principally to the responses of the students themselves. However, with the advent of competency-based assessment in the neoliberal era, practitioners felt that the very nature and purpose of accountability that had entered the policy discourse took no cognisance of the nature and purpose that the profession itself held for its accountability.

The community of practice that had characterised previous eras was fractured and, by the time of writing, was almost non-existent. With the marketisation of provision, the once unified field of ABE became a diverse range of fields of foundation skills with equally diverse communities of practice, each driven by top-down ideas of 'what matters' in terms of professional knowledge.

The concept of integration of literacy and numeracy into VET provision, which had begun in the 1990s, became the defining idea of LLN in the new millennium. Literacy and numeracy became everyone's business, and in the process, the specialist field of ABE became devalued and invisible.

Anne's final comment expressed the feelings of those interviewees who had experienced the vitality of the first two decades of the field and mourned its demise. When asked about the highs and lows of her career, she replied:

> And so, the concomitant low is right now, watching all that building work that was done in terms of resources, work force, academic programs, everything; watching it being explicitly and totally dismantled as we speak. I really think that many of us are grieving. All the other highs and lows pale into insignificance. (Interview)

References

ACAL1989, *Literacy: Let's get on with the job: Symposium report and discussion paper*, ACAL, Canberra.
ACAL1997, *Survey of aspects of literacy: Forum report*, ACAL, Canberra.
Acil Allen Consulting2015, *SEE programme evaluation*, Department of Education, Melbourne.
Anderson, D. 1996, 'The training market reforms and their impact on the vocational education and training system', paper presented to The Economic Impact of Vocational Education and Training, Centre for the Economics of Education and Training, Monash University.
Angus, L., Golding, B., Foley, F. & Lavender, P. 2013, 'Promoting "learner voice" in VET: Developing democratic, transformative possibilities or further entrenching the status quo?', *Journal of Vocational Education and Training* 65(4), 560–574.
Australian Industry Group2012, *When words fail: National workforce literacy project, final project report*, AIG, North Sydney.

Australian Industry Group2015, *Investing in workforce literacy pays*, AIG, North Sydney.

Australian Industry Group2016, *Tackling foundation skills in the workforce*, AIG, North Sydney.

Bair, J. 2015, 'Taking aim at the new international economic order', in P. Mirowski & D. Plehwe (eds), *The road from Mont Pèlerin: The making of the neoliberal thought collective*, Harvard University Press, Cambridge MA), 532–590.

Ball, S. & Junemann, C. 2018, *Networks, new governance and education*, The Policy Press, Bristol, UK.

Baynham, M. 1991, 'Literacy in TESOL and ABE: Exploring common themes', *Open Letter* 2(2), 4–16.

Black, S. 1995, *Literacy and the unemployed: Unemployed adult literacy students reflect on their referral by the CES to a literacy program and the role of literacy in their employment opportunities*, Centre for Language and Literacy, Faculty of Education, University of Technology, Sydney.

Black, S. 2010, 'Working the interstices: Adult basic education teachers respond to the audit culture', *Literacy and Numeracy Studies* 18(2), 6–25.

Black, S. & Yasukawa, K. 2016, 'Research that counts: OECD statistics and "policy entrepreneurs" impacting on Australian adult literacy and numeracy policy', *Research in Post-Compulsory Education* 21(3), 165–180.

Brock, P. 2001, 'Australia's language', in J. Lo Bianco & R. Wickert (eds), *Australian policy activism in language and literacy*, Language Australia, Melbourne, pp. 49–76.

Brown, T. 2006, 'From union inspired to industry led: How Australian Labor's training reform experiment turned sour', *Journal of Industrial Relations* 48(4), 491–505.

Callon, M. 1986, 'Some elements of a sociology of translation: Domestication of the scallops and the fishermen of St Brieuc Bay', in J. Law (ed.), *Power, action and belief: A new sociology of knowledge?*, Routledge and Kegan Paul, London.

Campbell, B. 2005, *Acting in the middle: The dialogic struggle for professional identity in adult literacy and basic education in Victoria*, Monash University, Victoria.

Campbell, B. 2009, *Reading the fine print – a history of the Victorian Adult Literacy and Basic Education Council (VALBEC) 1978–2008*, Victorian Adult Literacy and Basic Education Council, Springvale South.

Circelli, M. 2015, *Who is delivering foundation skills? A survey of the LLN and education and training workforces*, NCVER, Adelaide.

Coates, S., Fitzpatrick, L., McKenna, A. & Makin, A. 1995, *National Reporting System: A mechanism for reporting outcomes of adult English language, literacy and numeracy programs*, National Languages and Literacy Institute of Australia, Melbourne.

Courtenay, M. & Mawer, G. 1995, *Integrating English language, literacy and numeracy into vocational education and training: A framework – summary*, New South Wales Technical and Further Education Commission, Foundation Studies Training Division, Sydney.

A new discourse emerges 103

Darville, R. 2011, 'Unfolding the adult literacy regime', *Adult Education Research Conference*, University of Toronto Press, Toronto, pp. 163–169.
DEET1991, *Australia's language: The Australian Language and Literacy Policy*, AGPS, Canberra.
DESE2020, *Skills for Education and Employment (SEE) program*, https://docs.employment.gov.au/system/files/doc/other/see_eligibility_criteria_-_march_2020.pdf.
Falk, I. 2001, 'Sleight of hand: Job myths, literacy and social capital', in J. Lo Bianco & R. Wickert (eds), *Australian policy activism in language and literacy*, Language Australia, Melbourne, pp. 205–222.
Faure, E. 1972, *Learning to be: The world of education today and tomorrow*, UNESCO, Paris.
Gonczi, A. 2004, 'The new professional and vocational education', in G. Foley (ed.), *Dimensions of adult learning*, Allen and Unwin, Crows Nest, pp. 19–34.
Good, M. & Holmes, J. 1979, *How's it going? An alternative to testing students in adult literacy*, ALU, London.
Goodall, J. 2019, *The politics of the common good: Dispossession in Australia*, NewSouth, Sydney.
Goozee, G. 2001, *The development of TAFE in Australia*, NCVER, Adelaide.
Gribble, H. 1990, 'Resisting hijack and seduction', *Literacy Exchange, Journal of NSWALC* 2, 41–55.
Gribble, H. & Bottomley, J. 1989, *Some implications of award restructure proposals for adult literacy and basic education provision*, International Literacy Year Secretariat, Canberra.
Griffin, P. & Forwood, A. 1991, *Adult Literacy and Numeracy Competency Scales*, DEET, Canberra.
Hager, P. 2004, 'The competence affair, or why vocational education and training urgently needs a new understanding of learning', *Journal of Vocational Education and Training* 56(3), 409–433.
Hager, P. 2016, 'Bringing TAFE to its knees', *The Australian TAFE Teacher* 50(2), 18–20.
Hamilton, M. 2017, 'How international large-scale skills assessments engage with national actors: Mobilising networks through policy, media and public knowledge', *Critical Studies in Education* 58(3), 280–294.
Hamilton, M. & Barton, D. 2000, 'The International Adult Literacy Survey: What does it really measure?', *International Review of Education* 46(55), 377–389.
Hamilton, M. & Hillier, Y. 2006, *Changing faces of adult literacy, language and numeracy: A critical history*, Trentham Books, Stoke on Trent.
Hamilton, M., Macrae, C. & Tett, L. 2001, 'Powerful literacies: The policy context', in J. Crowther, M. Hamilton & L. Tett (eds), *Powerful literacies*, NIACE, Leicester.
Hammond, J. & Wickert, R. 1993, 'Pedagogical relations between adult ESL and adult literacy: Some directions for research', *Open Letter* 3(2), 16–31.

Hammond, J., Wickert, R., Burns, A. & Joyce, H. 1992, *The pedagogical relations between adult ESL and adult literacy*, UTS, Language and Literacy Centre, Sydney.

Harvey, D. 2005, *A brief history of neoliberalism*, Oxford University Press, New York.

Haughton, H. 2000, '"Good Practice" and "Fine Print"', *Literacy Link* 19(1), 6–7.

Hazell, P. 1998, *Student outcomes: Investigating competency-based curriculum in adult basic education*, University of Technology, Sydney.

IBSA2013, *Foundation Skills Training Package implementation guide*, Commonwealth of Australia, Canberra.

Industry Skills Council2011, *No more excuses: An industry response to the language, literacy and numeracy challenge*, ISC.

Johnston, B., Kelly, S. & Johnston, K. 2001, *The rise and fall of the NSW Adult Literacy and Information Office*, NSW ALNARC, Sydney.

Kell, P. 1999, 'The brave new world for literacy and numeracy: Markets, enterprises and mutual obligation', *Literacy Broadsheet* 52(April), 2–6.

Latour, B. 1987, *Science in action: How to follow scientists and engineers through society*, Harvard University Press, Cambridge, MA.

Limage, L. 2009, 'Multilateral cooperation for literacy promotion under stress: Governance and management issues ', *Literacy and Numeracy Studies* 17(2), 5–33.

Lo Bianco, J. 1999, *Globalisation: Frame word for education and training, human capital and human development/rights*, Language Australia, Melbourne.

Manwaring, K. & O'Maley, P. 2001, 'The Literacy and Numeracy Training Program: The journey thus far', *Fine Print* 24(1), 13–17.

Marginson, S. 1997, *Educating Australia – government, economy and citizen since 1960*, Cambridge University Press, Cambridge, England.

McKenna, R. & Fitzpatrick, L. 2004, *Building sustainable adult literacy provision: A review of international trends in adult literacy policy and programs – Support document*, NCVER, Adelaide, Australia.

Mirowski, P. 2015, 'Postface: Defining neoliberalism', in P. Mirowski & D. Plehwe (eds), *The road from Mont Pèlerin: The making of the neoliberal thought collective*, Harvard University Press, Cambridge, MA, pp. 609–667.

Mirowski, P. & Plehwe, D. (eds) 2015, *The road from Mont Pèlerin: The making of the neoliberal thought collective*, Harvard University Press, Cambridge, MA.

NALA2011, *A literature review of international adult literacy policies*, National Adult Literacy Agency, Dublin.

Nelson, A. 1985, *'The community development approach to literacy'*, paper presented to the Adult Literacy and Community Development Workshop, 19–25 August, Armidale.

NSW Adult Literacy & Numeracy Council2018, 'Response to PwC's case for change in the TAE training package', http://www.nswalnc.org.au/doc/Submission%20to%20PWC%20Skills%20for%20Australia_TAE_030418.pdf.

NSW Adult Literacy Council 1989, 'Conference resolutions', *Literacy Exchange* 1.
OECD 2000, *Literacy in the information age: Final report of the International Adult Literacy Survey*, OECD, Paris.
Osmond, P. 1989, 'The why, who, what and how of assessment', *Literacy Exchange* 2, 22–26.
Roberts, A. 2013, 'The Foundation Skills Training Package', *Fine Print* 36(1), 14–20.
Ryan, R. 2011, *How VET responds: A historical policy perspective*, NCVER, Adelaide.
Sanguinetti, J. 1999, 'Within and against performativity: Discursive engagement in adult literacy and basic education', PhD thesis, Deakin University, Victoria.
Sanguinetti, J. 2007, 'Meanings, traditions and contemporary policy discourse in adult literacy', *Literacy Link* 27(1), 6–8.
Sanguinetti, J. & Hartley, R. 2000, *Building literacy and numeracy into training: A synthesis of recent research into the effects of integrating literacy and numeracy into training packages*, Language Australia, Melbourne.
Schofield, K. 1994, 'The clash of the Titans', in P. Kearns & W. Hall (eds), *Kangan: 20 years on*, NCVER, Adelaide, pp. 57–77.
SCOTESE 2012, *National Foundation Skills Strategy for Adults*, Commonwealth of Australia, Canberra.
Seddon, T. 1994, 'Changing contexts – new debates: ALBE in the 1990s', *Open Letter* 5(1), 3–16.
Shipway, A. (ed.) 1988–1991, *Good practice in Australian adult literacy and basic education*, ALAC, Tasmania.
Shomos, A. 2010, *Links between literacy and numeracy skills and labour market outcomes*, Productivity Commission Staff Working Paper.
Sinclair, K.E. 1986, *Business Council of Australia report on education*, Business Council of Australia, Melbourne.
Skills Australia 2011, *Skills for prosperity: A roadmap for vocational education and training* Skills Australia, Canberra.
St Clair, R. 2012, 'The limits of levels: Understanding the International Adult Literacy Surveys (IALS)', *International Review of Education* 58(6), 759–776.
Stedman Jones, D. 2012, *Masters of the universe: Hayek, Friedman, and the birth of neoliberal politics*, Princeton University Press, Princeton, Oxford.
Street, B. 1990, 'Putting literacies on the political agenda', *Open Letter* 1(1), 5–15.
Tingle, L. 2015, 'Political amnesia: How we forgot to govern', *Quarterly Essay* 60, 6–75.
Tusting, K. 2009, '"I am not a 'good' teacher, I don't do all their paperwork": Teacher resistance to accountability demands in the English Skills for Life strategy', *Literacy and Numeracy Studies* 17(3), 6–26.
Wheelahan, L. 2016, 'Patching bits won't fix vocational education in Australia – a new model is needed', *International Journal of Training Research* 14(3), 180–196.

Wheelahan, L. & Moodie, G. 2011, *Rethinking skills in vocational education and training: From competencies to capabilities*, NSW Department of Education & Communities, Sydney.

Wickert, R., Searle, J., Marr, B. & Johnston, B. 2007, 'Opportunities, transitions and risks: Perspectives on adult literacy and numeracy development in Australia', *Review of Adult Learning and Literacy* 7(8), 245–284.

Wickert, R. & Zimmerman, J. 1991, 'Adult basic education in Australia: Questions of integrity', in M. Tennant (ed.), *Adult and continuing education in Australia: Issues and practices*, Routledge, London, pp. 175–206.

Wignall Consulting Services 2017, *The Framework: Foundation Skills Professional Standards Framework: version 1.1, June 2017*, Department of State Development, Adelaide, http://industryandskills.sa.gov.au/upload/fspsf/foundation-skills-professional-standards-framework.pdf.

Wignall, L. 1999, *Built in, not bolted on: Information kit for language, literacy and numeracy coordinators on incorporating communication skills into training packages*, ANTA, Melbourne.

Yasukawa, K. 2010, 'Breaking out of the package: Educating literacy and numeracy teachers with agency', *Literacy and Numeracy Studies* 18(2), 75–87.

Yasukawa, K. & Black, S. 2016, 'Policy making at a distance: A critical perspective on Australia's National Foundation Skills Strategy for Adults', in K. Yasukawa & S. Black (eds), *Beyond economic interests: Critical perspectives on adult literacy and numeracy in a globalised world*, Sense Publishers, Rotterdam, pp. 19–39.

Yasukawa, K., Hamilton, M. & Evans, J. 2017, 'A comparative analysis of national media responses to the OECD Survey of Adult Skills: Policy making from the global to the local?' *Compare* 47(2), 271–285.

Yeatman, A. 1993, 'Corporate managerialism and the shift from the welfare to the competition state', *Discourse: Studies in the Cultural Politics of Education* 13(2), 3–9.

Zimmerman, J. & Norton, M. 1990, 'The challenges for adult literacy in Australia', in J. D'Cruz & P. Langford (eds), *Issues in Australian education*, Longman Cheshire, Melbourne, pp. 144–168.

5 What have we learnt?
Some lessons from our history

Introduction

The first part of the narrative that I have traced detailed the genesis of the original humanist, adult basic education (ABE) discourse, and the programs that it produced. Their purpose was rooted in ideals of social justice; towards the 'complete fulfilment of man ... as individual, member of a family and of a community, citizen and producer, inventory of techniques and creative dreamer' (Faure 1972, p. vi). The previous chapter, however, showed that in the wake of the march of neoliberalism, and under the influence of a new and powerful group of influences on the actor network, those ideals have been lost from the public and policy discourse (although not entirely from the professional discourse). The role of ABE has been re-cast as being almost entirely in the service of the economy. In the public and policy sphere the human capital discourse has consistently eclipsed any appeals to 'the complete fulfilment of man' and his role in civil society.

In this chapter I consider what 'resources of hope' (Tett & Hamilton 2019) we might be able to muster as we attempt to re-problematise the project of ABE and to restore something of its moral purpose. I attempt to distil what lessons we might have learnt from our forty-year history, and to consider how we might apply them to the present context.

Although many interviewees suggested feelings of powerlessness and reluctance to engage in the counter-hegemonic project required to challenge the prevailing global socio-economic discourse, we are urged by others in the wider educational community to be courageous in our challenge to the common-sense appeal of the neoliberal argument; to challenge the dominant simplistic discourse of education as human capital; and to mobilise an alternate discourse (for example, Groundwater-Smith & Mockler 2009; Hamilton & Pitt 2011a, 2011b; Sumner 2008; Tett & Hamilton 2019). In the field of ABE, this alternate discourse implies one that includes at least some elements of the Adult Literacy Discourse to which practitioners have clung, even to the present era. It includes ideals of social justice, of humanist, student-centred education and literacy as social capital, of diversity of provision in order to meet the diversity of student needs, as well as critical theory's discourse of emancipation.

A search for green shoots

In spite of the pessimism that surrounds many teachers' reflections, there are many lessons to be learnt from our history that we might apply to the contemporary context. Perhaps the principal lesson to be learnt is that economic and political shifts, particularly those that are global in origin, have been deeply resistant to challenge. The hegemonic nature of the public discourse of imminent economic crisis, and the place that literacy has played in that discourse, has not been successfully challenged over the past three decades, in spite of the frustrations felt and voiced by those in the profession.

Concepts offered by policy theory suggest an explanation for this resistance. For example, Hanf discusses the concept of path dependency in institutional policy development. 'Once on a certain track, systems/institutions are bound to move on; they are shored up by positive feedback'(cited in Ryan 2011, p. 7). Ryan argues that the reason why VET policy in Australia (and beyond) has been immune to significant shifts in policy directions is that the political landscape of past thirty years has not produced significant upheavals, or 'policy windows' (p. 7), that may have ushered in a change from this policy path.

This perhaps explains the entrenched human capital discourse of the thirty years to the end of 2019. However, the global catastrophe created by the pandemic of 2020 has undoubtedly opened a future policy window, as the socio-economic settings of the future are, of necessity, re-calibrated. At the time of writing, it is hard to know what this long-term re-calibration will look like for social justice programs. It is, however, timely and in fact urgent for those who would argue for the creation of a more just society to make their voices heard.

Even before the economic tumult of 2020, there were signs in the global socio-economic landscape of small openings that could suggest a policy window for a change in discourse. These were not just voices from the left side of politics using the term neoliberalism as an 'intellectual swear word' (Mirowski & Plehwe 2015, p. 35). The neoliberal project had already come under increasing scrutiny from increasing members of the polity. We can perhaps take encouragement from the fact that there are many, many other socially progressive movements across the globe whose members are also questioning the very foundations of neoliberalism and the injustices and inequities that recent decades have wrought. Green shoots are emerging with a global demand for a more just world, with evidence of growing appeals to 'the better angels of our nature'. For example, the California-based Natural Capital Institute has developed a database of millions of 'civil society organisations from around the world directed to the issues of the environment and justice' (Hawken 2007, p. 191). Perhaps the best example of the mainstreaming of these ideals is the appearance on the New York Times Bestseller List of Hawken's book, a book that refers in its title to this collection of disparate social movements as 'the largest social movement in history' and describes the ways in which it is 'restoring grace, justice and beauty to the world' (Hawken 2007). He writes of these millions of nonprofit organisations that address issues such as social justice. Although they do not share common goals or ideologies or have a leader, as our conventional understanding of a movement would suggest, they share common values. In our appeal for a return to the social justice roots of our field, we can see ourselves as a part of this global movement.

The moral purpose

The interviewee comments that I have recorded here have demonstrated that teachers still search for a moral purpose in their teaching, towards 'the complete fulfilment of man'. They deeply resent the narrowness of the curricula that they are forced to interpret, and the lack of diversity of provision to meet the diversity of student needs. They also deeply resent the impact of the new compliance regime, brought about by the incursion of the mechanisms of corporate managerialism into the sphere of public education. It is clear also that complaints about the compliance requirements are not just about the work involved; the tension and frustration that most teachers express is with the conflict of discourses about what matters: doing the paperwork and being faithful to the curriculum or responding to students' needs (Tusting 2009).

There is, therefore, cause for optimism in the voices from practice that I have recounted here. Even in the recent era, with an educational context that teachers feel is hostile to the discourse of literacy as a human right, and to the ideals of student-centred pedagogy, practitioners cling to these ideals and many of the principles of the Adult Literacy Discourse. The archival data from this period and my 'stories from practice' indicate that many practitioners had never lost their belief in the social justice role of ABE and their concern for supporting literacy in its full social context. These remained issues of central concern in the professional discourse. For example, following an ACAL forum in 2003 titled 'Beyond training: locating literacy in social policy', forum organisers reflected that the forum had 'proved refreshing and exciting, reinvigorating the participants as social justice activists and reminding us what first drew us to the field' (Castleton & Foley 2003, p. 4).

In the previous chapter I referred to the ways in which teachers who were familiar with the Adult Literacy Discourse used diverse means to manipulate the current system to be able to bring some student-centred approaches to their pedagogy. The principles that underpinned the Adult Literacy Discourse of the foundation years, and that first drew them to the field, lingered in the minds of many. In reflecting on the current restrictions, Anne had this to say:

> All flexibility has gone. It feels like creativity in terms of being able to do what your students need [has gone]. We still try as teachers, we try terribly hard to do that, and to bend the words in the units of competence to reflect what we know our students need, because they tell us. It would be nice to be able to just do it without having to turn yourself inside out and bend over backwards and twist everything to give the students what they need. (Anne – interview)

There is ample evidence that, for many practitioners, their sense of the moral purpose of the task came as much from their personal values and attitudes as it did from the prevailing discourse and the curriculum documents they were required to negotiate and interpret. In Sonia's words, 'I actually want to make teaching an act of love rather than just a job' (Interview). These teachers made reference to student-centred approaches to teaching and learning springing from their own moral and professional judgement.

Nevertheless, a number of interviewees who had been active in the field in the years when the Adult Literacy Discourse was prevalent expressed concerns for teachers who were new to the field and who did not have access to the professional practice knowledge of the early community of practice. Sanguinetti (1999, p. 266) refers to these earlier practitioners as the 'culture carriers' of the pedagogical traditions of ABE. Sam referred to these 'culture carriers' as having within them a certain philosophy of operating, and I think that now anyone who comes in [to the profession] new isn't going to have that, and they are going to look at the training packages and they are going to look at the curriculum, and there is no one to tell them anything different from that so [the earlier philosophy] must dissipate. (Interview)

However, I found evidence from my 'stories from practice' that such concerns may be largely ill-founded. Even some of the interviewees who were new to the field and had only worked in contexts that were not sympathetic to the Adult Literacy Discourse referred to issues such as social justice as being the drivers of their practice.

Carolyn was one such teacher. She had only worked in the new context constrained by the human capital ideology and, when asked what she would like to see for the future of ABE, responded:

What about this scenario: if you had about 10 or 15 students and you had six months of 12 hours a week or something and it was completely over to you? It's a completely different paradigm isn't it, but it would be quite exciting, to sit down with those people at the beginning, and not really knowing where you're going to end up. (Interview)

She had conjured up a vision of student-centred practice reminiscent of the Adult Literacy Discourse: further evidence of 'green shoots' in the community of practice that are evident in the moral purpose that teachers still bring to the task. It was clear that issues of social justice still run through the professional discourse. The simple act of keeping this discourse alive is an act of resistance.

Acts of everyday resistance

My interviewees demonstrated overwhelming evidence of everyday resistance (Johansson & Vinthagen 2016) to the audit and compliance regime and a strong commitment to teaching that they believe has a moral purpose. Such acts of everyday resistance are displayed in statements such as 'Give me a box and I will tick it for you. I won't let it impinge on the way I teach. I won't do it' (Robyn – interview) and for many it required considerable effort to reconcile the compliance requirements of the new corporate managerialism with the needs of the students.

112 *What have we learnt?*

The frustration of attempting a student-centred approach in the face of these requirements was evident in the comments of many of these practitioners:

> I have been really impressed by how [teachers] have had to turn themselves backwards and inside out to actually try and still deliver a good product ... Because of course you still have to match those stupid outcomes and indicators ... The beauty of it is though, despite the curriculum and the training package and all that, people just keep doing what they were doing anyway. The cake's still the same, the icing just gets changed. (Jan – interview)

These statements demonstrate that even when the only delivery option was that of the Commonwealth-funded jobseeker program with its narrow work focussed learning outcomes, it seems that for many, pedagogy and professional practice changed little. *People just keep doing what they were doing anyway.* They protect their educational integrity by 'selectively ignoring' (Tusting 2009, p. 18) the dominant discourse as indicated in curriculum documents, demonstrating that in the eyes of many practitioners, the present policy discourse holds questionable legitimacy.

There is comfort also in the knowledge that this resistance to the dominant discourse is felt in similar countries; that there is a global community of practice; a 'thought collective' beset by similar policy constraints and producing similar acts of everyday resistance (for example, Bowl & Tobias 2012; Ramdeholl & Wells 2013; Tett & Hamilton 2019; Tusting 2009).

The future of VET

There is evidence also of growing unease and dissatisfaction with a source of much of the narrowness that has beset the field of ABE: that is, the interpretation of competency-based training that evolved in Australia, and that underpins the VET sector. There have been signs of a re-evaluation of the present interpretation of CBT and the concept of training packages that flowed from it. These concepts are now receiving revived critical analysis at more than just practitioner level (for example, Angus et al. 2013; Hager 2004, 2016; Wheelahan 2016; Wheelahan & Moodie 2011) and have been welcomed by practitioners such as my interviewees. As Lorraine, who was close to the VET policy discussions at the time, remarked:

Just in the last couple of years the Commonwealth and the State have commissioned enquiries into the limitations of training products. Lisa Wheelahan ... is promoting a 'think about capabilities approach'. So, I think that there could be an opportunity to say, at the moment, it is not working so let's look at something different ... I don't know if we are there yet, but it is nice to hear in public forums. It's kind of something to build on. (Lorraine – interview)

Perhaps we are 'not there yet', but the argument for the fundamental inappropriateness of CBT for language, literacy and numeracy development should be a central proposition in the VET sector's inevitable discussion of changes to CBT, presenting an important opportunity for literacy activists. Such discussions are reminiscent of similar discussions in the early 1990s (Gribble 1990; Wickert & Zimmerman 1991), when ABE activists argued that transferring ABE's body of 'just and enlightening' professional practice knowledge to the mainstream of VET was not going to be easy, but that abandoning it would not lead to the development of the flexible, critically thinking workers that the new industrial environment would require.

Some lessons from our history

Immutable mobiles

I have represented UNESCO's *Learning to be* (Faure 1972), and subsequently the OECD's international L/N skills surveys (OECD 2000) as the *immutable mobiles* of the past. A new potential *immutable mobile* appeared in 2016 with the international community's adoption of the 2030 goals of the *Agenda for Sustainable Development*. Of particular interest is Sustainable Development Goal (SDG) 4 (UNESCO 2016) which laid out a vision to:

> Ensure inclusive and equitable quality education and promote lifelong learning opportunities for all ... It is inspired by a humanistic vision of education and development based on human rights and dignity; social justice; inclusion; protection; cultural, linguistic and ethnic diversity; and shared responsibility and accountability. We reaffirm that education is a public good, a fundamental human right and a basis for guaranteeing the realization of other rights. It is essential for peace, tolerance, human fulfilment and sustainable development. (p. 7)

These words echo the 1972 discourse of *Learning to be*; words that can be used by the ABE community to invoke authority for a return to a discourse of humanist education and to a vision of education as a shared good. However, our history tells us that enlightened and visionary statements such as these mean little if governments do not directly act on them, since the market will not. These words, and these documents are inevitably open to a range of interpretations. *Agenda for Sustainable Development* goes on to present the concept of lifelong learning as an individual responsibility with little reference to the systemic inequalities that mitigate against 'inclusive and equitable quality education'. There is little in the document to encourage governments to invest in education as an instrument in the promotion of equality. A critical reading of documents such as this can reveal them as neoliberalism-lite; the words mask a continued bias in favour of the utilitarian, human capital, instrumentalist vision of learning (see, for example Vargas-Tamez 2019; Walker 2009). Nevertheless, it articulates a goal that ABE activists might take as an authoritative starting point to argue for a re-imagined field of lifelong education, education that aims not only to help students 'read the word', but also to 'read the world' (Freire & Macedo 1987).

Human actors

The early part of this narrative referred to many human actors in the actor network; these were individual bureaucrats, members of parliament and organisation managers, who were referred to in the archival record as 'good friends of adult literacy'. They were joined by members of the community of practice, both individually and collectively, with each playing a strong and identifiable role in the development of policy.

The later part of the narrative records the influence of fewer of these individual human actors. They had been sidelined by the juggernaut of neoliberalism and the entities that promoted a narrow interpretation of its ideology. The role of government had changed, distancing it from the citizenry. The days of 'insider policy activists' being invited to work alongside bureaucrats in the development of policy had long passed.

There are, however, many 'good friends of adult literacy' still in positions of some influence. They reside now not only in government and the bureaucracy, but in the plethora of quasi-governmental entities that act in partnership with government and wield strong influence on public policy. The network of actors has changed, but the advice of Arch Nelson on the importance of lobbying and making use of people in power is as important now as it was in the late 1970s, albeit with more difficulty.

Diversity of provision

The story that I have told is one that has traditionally been conceived in terms of institutional course provision within the VET system. Many of my interviewees suggested, however, that it may be time to re-imagine what the field might look like, and what its boundaries might be. It may be time to reconsider the 1975 recommendation of the Richardson Committee that 'an effective literacy program will almost certainly have to be conducted outside the formal institutional framework' (Richardson 1975, p. 96), a recommendation that was heeded for only a brief time.

I have suggested that the decision to place the field within the responsibility of the VET sector has had unforeseen and unwanted consequences by narrowing the value placed on ABE to an instrumental and vocational one. Rose's warning words in relation to adult education in USA can be read also as a warning for adult educators and policy makers in Australia:

> The de facto philosophy of education we do have is a strictly economic one. This is dangerous for without a civic and moral core it could easily lead to a snazzy twenty-first-century version of an old and shameful pattern in American education: working class people get a functional education geared only toward the world of work. (Rose 2012, p. 141)

Anne's description of provision during 'Australia's literacy decade' referred to *literacy teachers ... setting up classes here, there and everywhere*. These were classes set up in TAFE colleges and in community settings; for students with vocational needs and for others with personal and social needs; they were facilitated by professional, specialist teachers and also by volunteer tutor programs. In short, they aimed at providing a diversity of provision to meet the diversity of adult needs. With the urgency to attach the value of literacy to the human capital discourse, this diversity of provision became lost, and the opportunities to provide a lifelong basic education for all adults is lost also. Not only do jobseeker foundation skills programs serve only a minority of adults who are seeking to improve their literacy and numeracy skills, the short, quick fix of these programs ignores the reality of literacy development, that such programs provide only limited gains in proficiency. Sustained gains are most likely to result from continued engagement with literacy practices (Reder 2013), suggesting the necessity for provision of a wide range of ABE programs for adults to dip into in their quest for a lifelong education. Many Australian ABE practitioners would agree with Reder's assessment of the field in USA, that 'adult literacy education needs to be repositioned within a new framework of lifelong and life-wide learning, a framework in which new policies are formulated, programs are designed and evaluated, and research is funded and carried out' (Reder 2020, p. 48).

Perhaps it is time to argue for additional sites of provision outside of the VET institutional provision, so that adults with other goals might be accommodated, along with those whose complex lives do not fit well with institutionalised provision (Barton et al. 2007). Several of my interviewees mentioned the growth of interest coming from some community libraries and a suggestion was made of a widening of the possible role for libraries or other community facilities, making reference to Levine's (1986) suggestion of a drop-in centre which could act as a hub for a variety of literacy activity. Arch Nelson's proposition that 'unless a move for literacy is community based, it is unlikely to succeed' (Nelson 1985, p. 31) is a warning from the past.

The way forward

A new thought collective

Finding allies in this struggle to regain something of our social justice roots requires us to identify some fellow travellers amongst the disparate social movements referred to above. We are reminded of Mirowski's description of the master neoliberals' 'thought collectives': interdisciplinary collections of individuals and groups of journalists, politicians, academics and corporate leaders (Mirowski & Plehwe 2015, pp. 31–32) who were tasked with spreading the early ideas and ideology of neoliberalism. They represented the actor network that the master neoliberals consciously developed around their discourse, and that are represented still in the actor network responsible for redefining the ABE discourse in narrow instrumentalist, human capital terms. They include representatives of industry who were urged to 'sing from the same hymn sheet' (cited in Yasukawa & Black 2016), a hymn sheet that became a very powerful anthem for industry lobbies (for example, Australian Industry Group 2015, 2016; Shomos 2010; Skills Australia 2011).

In the same way, ABE practitioners and activists might also build solidarity with others who share their core social justice values (Yasukawa & Osmond 2019). New discursive spaces will need to be created and associations with other social justice movements forged with an alternative hymn sheet to sing from. A new counter-hegemonic bloc of actors is needed.

Re-professionalising the profession

The previous chapter referred to the fact that the 1990s had been called 'Australia's literacy decade' (McKenna & Fitzpatrick 2004, p. 66), a period that brought with it the professionalisation of ABE, with a specialist trained workforce. Ironically, by the end of that period many in the profession felt that they had lost control of the agenda, since that period also coincided with the intensification of the tools of corporate managerialism, including, for ABE, the outsourcing of many of the tools of the profession, such as development of the curricula and assessment protocols. The body of professional practice knowledge that had been created by the ABE community of practice in the foundation years was replaced by a body of professional practice knowledge imposed from above, from the new actors in the actor network. Government-funded programs were required to employ curricula that exclusively specified outcomes 'for work'. Specialist ABE qualifications were no longer demanded, so that tertiary institutions no longer offered them. The profession became de-professionalised. ABE teachers became trainers and adult education morphed into employment skills development.

Professionalism suggests trust, autonomy and agency, values that were evident in the foundation era with its creative and vibrant community of practice, all fed by professional development and research. In those days of government investment in education these activities were all supported by government infrastructure and funding. That infrastructure no longer exists, so that in order for practitioners to reclaim some of the shared professional practice of the past, and to critically analyse what the future might look like, those communities of practice will need to be strengthened from within.

Research

My collection of archival materials, and a brief literature search attests to the plethora of research that was produced during Australia's Literacy Decade, research that was supported by tertiary institutions and the government infrastructure and funding that the field enjoyed in that period. This was research that fed the scholarly underpinning of the field's professional practice knowledge, but that faded with the entry to the actor network of the new creators of the public and policy discourse: employer bodies, industry lobby groups and organisations with easy and direct access to government and to resources to fund research that demonstrated their argument: that is, the link between levels of literacy and economic prosperity. The research that found sponsors in this period is 'research *for* policy' (Lingard 2013), that is, research that is designed to legitimate certain policy directions promoted by the research sponsors, rather than research that would suggest or lead policy and practice.

One contribution that present practitioners might make to balance this body of research is the promotion of a climate of practitioner inquiry (see, for example, Duckworth & Hamilton 2016). This would help to illuminate once again the professional practice knowledge of the field and add nuance to the current narrowly focussed research promoted by those bodies whose interest lies in the human capital argument.

Adding nuance to the public imaginary

One avenue of such participant research is the analysis and publication of student stories. These stories insert an alternative narrative into the public imaginary: one that relates to the lived experience and needs of those adults who are not necessarily served by the human capital agendas, but whose lives and communities could be enriched by access to ABE provision.

ABE teachers are the custodians of a wealth of student stories that testify to the need for adult education that addresses the whole person, not only the jobseeker or worker in that person. The practice of publishing student written stories, which was prevalent in the foundation years, continues in a limited way still. For example, the collection of UK and Australian stories of *Resilience: Stories of adult learning* (Furlong & Yasukawa 2016, p. 3) demonstrate 'the critical role of lifelong learning, and how adult literacies weave through our journeys, visibly and invisibly'. ABE classrooms and staffrooms are replete with these stories; stories that should rightly find their way into the public discourse also. In these more stringent times, the digital space provides opportunity for the telling and sharing of student stories (see, for example, Duckworth & Smith 2019).

A further opportunity to add nuance to the public discourse is presented with the survey results from the OECD's PIAAC survey that appear regularly in the public and policy discourse. Most public discussions around adult literacy in Australia invariably produce statements such as '44 per cent of Australia's population' have inadequate literacy skills; a statistic reported in *Australia's National Foundation Skills Strategy* (SCOTESE 2012, p. 1) and uncritically repeated as the *immutable mobile* to inform any argument. There is an opportunity not only to interrogate the implications of this statistic but also to add something of the wealth of data related to public and civic participation that is produced by these surveys but that remain un-examined in the public and policy sphere; a further opportunity to present literacy as a social practice, with its full range of values.

Concluding remarks

I am conscious that in many ways I have not been able to avoid a sense of celebration of and nostalgia about the earlier years of the field and the Adult Literacy Discourse that it produced. Whilst this discourse was a product of its time, and one that cannot be reproduced in the present climate, or even a re-calibration of the present climate, I cannot distance myself from the sentiment of many of my interviewees who mourn its demise, and agree with Jan that:

> I hope it rises again in a strengthened, different form. It will rise, but it will be different. ... But the world as we know it or knew it is gone. It's well and truly gone, and I am just absolutely grateful that I was there for the best of it. It was a privilege, we had good people and good ideas and a worthwhile thing to be doing. Absolute privilege. (Interview)

References

Angus, L., Golding, B., Foley, F. & Lavender, P. 2013, 'Promoting "learner voice" in VET: developing democratic, transformative possibilities or further entrenching the status quo?', *Journal of Vocational Education and Training* 65(4), 560–574.
Australian Industry Group 2015, *Investing in workforce literacy pays*, AIG, North Sydney.
Australian Industry Group 2016, *Tackling foundation skills in the workforce*, AIG, North Sydney.
Barton, D., Ivanič, R., Appleby, Y., Hodge, R. & Tusting, K. 2007, *Literacy, lives and learning*, Routledge, London.
Bowl, M. & Tobias, R. 2012, 'Learning from the past, organizing for the future: Adult and community education in Aotearoa New Zealand', *Adult Education Quarterly* 62(3), 272–286.
Castleton, G. & Foley, H. 2003, 'Tasmanian forum report – beyond training: Locating literacy in social policy', *Literacy Link* 23(3), 4.
Duckworth, V. & Hamilton, M. 2016, 'The significance of research and practice in adult literacy in the UK', in K. Yasukawa & S. Black (eds), *Beyond*

economic interests: Critical perspectives on adult literacy and numeracy in a globalised world, Sense, Rotterdam, pp. 167–184.

Duckworth, V. & Smith, R. 2019, 'Research, adult literacy and criticality: Catalysing hope and dialogic caring', in L. Tett & M. Hamilton (eds), Resisting neoliberalism in education: Local, national and transnational perspectives, Policy Press, Bristol, UK, pp. 27–40.

Faure, E. 1972, Learning to be: The world of education today and tomorrow, UNESCO, Paris.

Freire, P. & Macedo, D. 1987, Literacy: Reading the word and the world, Routledge and Kegan Paul, London.

Furlong, T. & Yasukawa, K. (eds) 2016, Resilience: Stories of adult learning, RaPAL/ACAL, Rolleston on Dove, England.

Gribble, H. 1990, 'Resisting hijack and seduction', Literacy Exchange, Journal of NSWALC 2, 41–55.

Groundwater-Smith, S. & Mockler, N. 2009, Teacher professional learning in an age of compliance: Mind the gap, Dordrecht, Springer.

Hager, P. 2004, 'The competence affair, or why vocational education and training urgently needs a new understanding of learning', Journal of Vocational Education and Training 56(3), 409–433.

Hager, P. 2016, 'Bringing TAFE to its knees', The Australian TAFE Teacher 50 (2), 18–20.

Hamilton, M. & Pitt, K. 2011a, 'Challenging representations: constructing the adult literacy learners over 30 years of policy and practice in the United Kingdom', Reading Research Quarterly 46(4), 350–373.

Hamilton, M. & Pitt, K. 2011b, 'Changing policy discourses: Constructing literacy inequalities', International Journal of Educational Development 31(6), 596–605.

Hawken, P. 2007, Blessed unrest: How the largest social movement in history is restoring grace, justice, and beauty to the world, Penguin, New York.

Johansson, A. & Vinthagen, S. 2016, 'Dimensions of everyday resistance: An analytical framework', Critical Sociology 42(3), 417–435.

Levine, K. 1986, The social context of literacy, Routledge and Kegan Paul, London.

Lingard, B. 2013, 'The impact of research on education policy in an era of evidence-based policy', Critical Studies in Education 54(2), 113–131.

McKenna, R. & Fitzpatrick, L. 2004, Building sustainable adult literacy provision: A review of international trends in adult literacy policy and programs – Support document, NCVER, Adelaide, Australia.

Mirowski, P. & Plehwe, D. (eds) 2015, The road from Mont Pèlerin: The making of the neoliberal thought collective, Harvard University Press, Cambridge, MA.

Nelson, A. 1985, 'The community development approach to literacy', paper presented to the Adult Literacy and Community Development Workshop, 19–25 August, Armidale.

OECD 2000, *Literacy in the information age: Final report of the International Adult Literacy Survey*, OECD, Paris.

Ramdeholl, D. & Wells, R. 2013, '*Against the grain: Oral histories from adult literacy workers in New York City*', paper presented to the National Conference of the Canadian Association for the Study of Adult Education, University of Victoria, British Columbia, 3–5 June.

Reder, S. 2013 'Lifelong and life-wide adult literacy development', *Perspectives on Language and Literacy* 39(2), 18–21.

Reder, S. 2020, 'A lifelong and life-wide framework for adult literacy education', *Adult Literacy Education* 2(1), 48–53.

Richardson, E.C. 1975, *TAFE in Australia: Second report on needs in technical and further education*, AGPS, Canberra.

Rose, M. 2012, *Back to school*, The New Press, New York.

Ryan, R. 2011, *How VET responds: A historical policy perspective*, NCVER, Adelaide.

Sanguinetti, J. 1999, 'Within and against performativity: Discursive engagement in adult literacy and basic education', PhD thesis, Deakin University, Victoria.

SCOTESE 2012, *National Foundation Skills Strategy for Adults*, Commonwealth of Australia, Canberra.

Shomos, A. 2010, *Links between literacy and numeracy skills and labour market outcomes* Productivity Commission Staff Working Paper, Canberra.

Skills Australia 2011, *Skills for prosperity: A roadmap for vocational education and training* Skills Australia, Canberra.

Sumner, J. 2008, 'Governance, globalization, and political economy', *Adult Education Quarterly* 59(1), 22–41.

Tett, L. & Hamilton, M. (eds) 2019, *Resisting neoliberalism in education: Local, national and transnational perspectives*, Policy Press, Bristol, UK.

Tusting, K. 2009, '"I am not a 'good' teacher, I don't do all their paperwork": Teacher resistance to accountability demands in the English Skills for Life strategy', *Literacy and Numeracy Studies* 17(3), 6–26.

UNESCO 2016, *Education 2030 Incheon declaration and framework for action for the implementation of sustainable development goal 4*, UNESCO, Paris.

Vargas-Tamez, C. 2019, 'Leaving no one behind: Bringing equity and inclusion back into education', in L. Tett & M. Hamilton (eds), *Resisting neoliberalism in education*, Policy Press, Bristol), 239–252.

Walker, J. 2009, 'The inclusion and construction of the worthy citizen through lifelong learning: A focus on the OECD', *Journal of Education Policy* 24(3), 335–351.

Wheelahan, L. 2016, 'Patching bits won't fix vocational education in Australia – a new model is needed', *International Journal of Training Research* 14(3), 180–196.

Wheelahan, L. & Moodie, G. 2011, *Rethinking skills in vocational education and training: From competencies to capabilities*, NSW Department of Education & Communities, Sydney.

Wickert, R. & Zimmerman, J. 1991, 'Adult basic education in Australia: Questions of integrity', in M. Tennant (ed.), *Adult and continuing education in Australia: Issues and practices*, Routledge, London, pp. 175–206.

Yasukawa, K. & Black, S. 2016, 'Policy making at a distance: A critical perspective on Australia's National Foundation Skills Strategy for Adults', in K. Yasukawa & S. Black (eds), *Beyond economic interests: Critical perspectives on adult literacy and numeracy in a globalised world*, Sense Publishers, Rotterdam, pp. 19–39.

Yasukawa, K. & Osmond, P. 2019, 'Adult basic education in Australia: In need of a new song sheet?', in L. Tett & M. Hamilton (eds), *Resisting neoliberalism in education: Local, national and transnational perspectives*, Policy Press, Bristol, UK, pp. 195–207.

Index

accredited curriculum 46–47
Active Employment Strategy 81
Actor Network Theory (ANT) 12–14, 32
Adult and Community Education (ACE) 94
adult basic education (ABE) 5, 10–12, 20, 45, 48, 54, 61–62; in Australia 78–99; community of practice 94–99; deprofessionalising the profession 93–94; future of VET 112–113; integration 87–89; literacy/numeracy actor network 92; national policy 80–87; national strategy 91–92; outsourced foundation skills products 89–91; overview 107–108; purpose 109–111; resistance 111–112; *see also* adult literacy; capitals; NSW adult basic education programs
adult education 1–2, 4, 23–24, 28, 34–35, 38, 42, 44, 46, 62, 65, 87, 115, 117–118
adult literacy 2–4; 1970 period 17; defined 5; early literacy programs 24–25; election of Whitlam government 20; field for 17–25; Freire, P. 23–24; legacy 24–25; in NSW 4; overview 17; post-war Australia 20; terminology 5; UNESCO 18–19; vocational education and training (VET) 20–23

Adult Literacy Action Campaign (ALAC) 54
Adult Literacy and Community Development (Nelson and Dymock) 34
adult literacy discourse 33–39; emancipation 38–39; participation 36–38; personal growth 35–36; principles 33; self-direction 34–35; social capital 39; student-centred 33–34
Adult Literacy Information Office (ALIO) 40, 47–49, 98–99
Adult Literacy Resource Agency (ALRA) 29, 47, 52
advocacy groups, emergence of 28–31
agency 52–53
Anglophone nations 1
Australian actors coalition 67–70
Australian Association for Adult Education (AAAE) 28
Australian Bureau of Statistics (ABS) 8
Australian Committee on Technical and Further Education (ACOTAFE) 21, 22
Australian Council for Adult Literacy (ACAL) 5, 11, 28–31, 84
Australian Language and Literacy Policy (ALLP) 80–81
Australian microeconomic reform 68–70
Australian National Training Authority (ANTA) 79

Index

Baynham, M. 86
Black, S. 7–8, 66, 71, 75, 78, 81–82, 92, 116
Board of Adult Education (BAE) 31–32
Britain 5, 42, 47

Cadman, A. 20, 23, 52–53
Cadman Report 23
Callon, M. 13
Canada 83
capitals 6; human 6–8; identity 8–9; social 8
case study 3–4
Certificate of Adult Basic Education (CABE) 46–47
Charnley, A. 5, 56
class-based tuition 43–44
coalition of actors 62
collaboration 50–51
Commonwealth Employment Service (CES) 81, 83
Commonwealth Government 31, 48
Commonwealth of Australia 4
Commonwealth Tertiary Education Commission (CTEC) 45
community development approach to literacy, The (Nelson) 29
community of practice 49–52, 94–99
community programs 2
Competency-Based Training (CBT) 72–74
Côté, J. 8
culture carriers 110–111

deletion 13
Department of Technical and Further Education (TAFE) 9, 11–12
deprofessionalising the profession 93–94
Devereux, B. 29
discourse emerges 61–101; adult basic education (ABE) in Australia 78–99; coalition of actors on global stage 62; coalition of Australian actors 67–70; human capital ideology 64–65; *immutable mobile* 65–67; market liberal economics 62–63; media 66–67; New Right 64; OECD 64–67; overview 61–62; VET in Australia 70–78
Dymock, D. 24, 34–35, 56

education, moral purpose 3, 107–109, 112–117, 118
emancipation, adult literacy discourse 38–39
English for Speakers of Other Languages (ESOL) 10, 86
enrolment 13

Falkenmire, G. 24–25, 32
Field, J. 8
First World War 63
forced marriage 86–87
Foundation Skills 5, 92
Foundation Skills Professional Standards Framework 93
Foundation Skills Training Package (FSK) 90
foundation years 28–57; adult literacy discourse 33–39; Adult Literacy Information Office (ALIO) 47–49; advocacy groups, emergence of 28–31; agency 52–53; Australian Council for Adult Literacy (ACAL) 29–31; Commonwealth Government involvement 31; community of practice 49–52; *National Policy on Languages* (NPL) 54–56; NSW, development 31–32; NSW adult basic education programs 40–47; overview 28
Freire, P. 23–24, 36–37, 42–43
Friedman, M. 63

Goodall, J. 63
Good practice in Australian literacy and basic education (Shipway) 34, 98
government role 69–70
Graff, H. J. 7, 15
Gribble, H. 36, 43, 45, 79

Hamilton, M. 4–7, 10, 12–13, 28, 65–66, 107, 112, 118
Hammond, J. 87
Hayek, F. A. 63
Henry, K. 70

Index 125

human actors 114
human capital 6–8, 19
human capital ideology 64–65
human rights 17

identity capital 8–9
Illich, I. 36
immutable mobiles 18, 22, 65–67, 113–114
Industry Training Advisory Bodies (ITABS) 88
Institute of Technical and Adult Teacher Education 44
integration, ABE 87–89
International Adult Literacy Survey (IALS) 65
International Labour Organization (ILO) 21
International Literacy Year (ILY) 84

jobseeker 81–84, 94, 112, 115, 118
Johnston, B. 99
Jones, H. 5, 56
Jungeblut, A. 55
Jurmo, P. 36

Kangan, M. 20–22, 28, 31, 71–72
Kangan Report 21–22
Kebby, H. 46
Kirsch, I. 55

labour market 9
language, literacy and numeracy (LLN) 68–70, 75–76, 83, 86, 88–89, 92, 97
Learning to be (Faure) 18, 21, 66, 113–114
Lee, A. 33, 36, 38
literacy: defined 5–6; the social practice view 5–6; the autonomous view 25; myths 7; *see also* adult literacy
Literacy and Numeracy Exchange 36–37, 96
Literacy and Numeracy Training (LANT) 82–83
Literacy in the Information Age (OECD) 66
Literacy Myth, The (Graff) 7

literacy/numeracy actor network 92
Lo Bianco, J. 18, 54, 75

market liberal economics 62–63
media 66–67
mobilisation 13
moment 13

National Foundation Skills Strategy Project 91, 93
National Policy on Languages (NPL) 54–56
National Training Reform Agenda (NTRA) 72
Nelson, A. 28–29, 84, 114
neoliberalism 1, 4, 62–63, 107–109, 114, 116
New Right 64, 69
New South Wales (NSW) 4, 9, 11, 23–24, 29, 31–32
NSW adult basic education programs 40–47
NSW Adult Literacy Council (NSWALC) 31, 37, 45, 48, 55
NSW Adult Migrant English Service (AMES) 31
numeracy skills 8

OECD *see* Organisation for Economic Co-operation and Development (OECD)
Organisation for Economic Co-operation and Development (OECD) 8, 21, 64–67
Outcomes of Adult Literacy Programs (Brennan, Clark and Dymock) 55–56
outsourced foundation skills products 89–91

partial translation 79
participation, adult literacy discourse 36–38
pedagogy 49
Penglase, B. 24
personal growth, adult literacy discourse 35–36
post-secondary education 4
post-war Australia 20
PricewaterhouseCoopers (PwC) 90

Index

problematisation 13
professional development 51
Programme for the International Assessment of Adult Competencies (PIAAC) 65, 67
provision diversity 42–45
public imaginary 118–119

Reading Writing Hotline 11
reports: *Cadman Report* 23; *Kangan Report* 21–22; *Richardson Report* 22–23
re-professionalising the profession 117
research 117–118
Research and Practice in Adult Literacy (RaPAL) 11
Resilience: Stories of adult learning (Furlong and Yasukawa) 11
Richardson, E. C. 20, 28, 31, 40, 48
Richardson Report 22–23

Sanguinetti, J. 110
Schuller, T. 6, 8–9
Seddon, T. 79
self-direction, adult literacy discourse 34–35
skills: foundation 5; numeracy 8; training 5
Skills for Education and Employment (SEE) 83
social capital 8, 39
social consciousness 17
social justice 1, 3–6, 18–19, 20, 31, 56, 57, 64–65, 80, 82, 100, 107–111, 113, 116
Special Intervention Program (SIP) 81
Street, B. 4, 6, 24–25, 68
student-centred, adult literacy discourse 33–34
student-centred adult literacy 2
students, described 9–11
Sustainable Development Goal (SDG) 113

TAFE Adult Basic Education program 32
TAFE in Australia (Kangan) 21
TAFE NSW adult basic education program 40–42

TAFE Teachers Association (TAFE TA) 44
Teaching English as a Second or Other Language (TESOL) 10
Technical and Further Education (TAFE) 9, 11–12, 21–25, 31, 37, 40, 48
tensions 44–45
terminology 4–9; adult basic education (ABE) 5; adult literacy 5
Tobin, T. 41
Training and Assessment (TAE) 89–90
training market, VET 78
translation 13–14

United Nations Educational, Scientific and Cultural Organization (UNESCO) 5, 10, 18–19, 64–65; human capital 19; social justice 18–19
Universal Declaration of Human Rights, The (United Nations) 18
University of Technology Sydney (UTS) 96
USA 5

vocational education and training (VET) 9, 20–23, 40, 45, 61, 68, 70–78, 90; assessment 74–78; Competency-Based Training (CBT) 72–74; future of 112–113; influence of industry 71; National Training Reform Agenda (NTRA) 72; training market 78
volunteer tutor program 42–43

White, K. 12, 23, 36–37, 39, 41, 43, 45, 47–49, 52
Whitlam government election 20
Wickert, R. 12, 32–33, 36, 38, 55, 76, 80, 87
workplace 84–86
Workplace English Language and Literacy (WELL) 84

Yasukawa, K. 7–8, 11, 66, 71, 90, 92, 116, 118

Zimmerman, J. 55, 80

For Product Safety Concerns and Information please contact our EU representative GPSR@taylorandfrancis.com
Taylor & Francis Verlag GmbH, Kaufingerstraße 24, 80331 München, Germany

www.ingramcontent.com/pod-product-compliance
Lightning Source LLC
Chambersburg PA
CBHW070738230426
43669CB00014B/2502